S A I N T S

S A I N T S

THEIR CULTS AND ORIGINS

CAROLINE WILLIAMS

BERGSTROM+BOYLE BOOKS   LONDON

Contents

Produced and published by
Bergström + Boyle Books Limited
31 Foubert's Place, London W1V 1HE
Printed and bound in Hong Kong by
Mandarin Offset International Limited
Production Services by
Book Production Consultants, Cambridge

ISBN 0 903767 33 3 (hardback)
ISBN 0 903767 28 7 (paperback)

Preface   7

Introduction   8

Apostles and Evangelists   11

Martyrs   23

Virgin Martyrs   33

Theologians   43

Virgin Penitents
and Fallen Women   53

Visionaries and Mystics   63

Monastics   73

Founders   83

Missionaries   93

Leaders and Heroes   107

Index   112

Cover picture: **St Aloysius Gonzaga** (contemporary plastic statuette, photograph by Theo Bergstrom)

1. St Joseph with the Christ Child (contemporary stoup) St Joseph is honoured as the foster father of Jesus Christ and protector of the Virgin Mary. He is the patron of carpenters, house-hunters and of the universal church. His symbol is the lily of purity.

2. Scene from the Life of St Wenceslas (Master of the School of Litomeice) The Good King Wenceslas of the carol, he was murdered by his brother Boleslav's supporters.

3. The Descent from the Cross (Rembrandt) St Joseph of Arimathaea obtained permission from Pontius Pilate to remove and bury Christ's body. He is the patron of undertakers.

4. The Saint and the Hero (Tenniel) Published during the Risorgimento, Garibaldi is dismissing a petulant saint who is carrying the blood of St Januarius, a relic still preserved in Naples Cathedral which liquefies at certain times of the year. This phenomenon has been carefully recorded for five centuries.

Preface

Children do not like to wear spectacles and I was no exception. From the age of four I was the unwilling wearer of those standard pink ones and demonstrated my loathing of them by hanging them on the bushes and fences in the garden and then telling my mother that I had lost them. She would send me to look for them, often with the words, 'Ask St Anthony to help you find them.' Thirty years later I was surprised to notice that I was still automatically muttering to myself, '*Please* St Anthony, help me find my damned specs.'

During eleven years in a trio of Catholic convents I found that St Anthony of Padua was only one of many saints who cropped up during the course of the day. On almost every day of the year at least one saint was specially honoured. All the rooms in the convents boasted one or more religious images so the heavenly and saintly faces were as familiar as those of the royal family or favourite film stars. I felt that it was unfair that I should lack a holy namesake; there is no St Caroline.

The influence of a convent upbringing will always affect me and as I began to research the lives of those saints whom I felt I could now recognise as historic figures instead of ever-present goads to self-improvement, I wondered how and why they had been venerated. My choice is random and personal; the saints described and illustrated in this book display a wide range of human reactions to religious conditioning.

BOUASSE-LEBEL & FILS & MASSIN   M.132   29, RUE ST SULPICE, PARIS

S? ANTOINE DE PADOUE,
PRIEZ POUR NOUS.

5. St Anthony of Padua, known as 'The Hammer of the Heretics', was a Portuguese Franciscan of the thirteenth century, whose assistance is invoked in finding lost articles.

Introduction

History has repeatedly shown that monotheism can be too demanding and uncomfortable a belief for the ordinary worshipper. Evolved from the Judaic and Greek traditions, Christianity instituted the concept of the Holy Trinity and accepted the paradox of Christ's dual nature – his earthly and his heavenly existence. Later Christians further increased the divine population by creating and venerating a communion of saints who, by their earthly lives, enabled the faithful to focus and channel their own religious energies and aspirations. They were more immediate, more accessible – intermediaries who might plead a supplicant's cause with a distant and awful God. It is probable that such veneration of heroes also fulfils a more primitive urge of ancestor worship.

A saint is a person of holy character who is venerated as an example of religious and personal excellence for having lived a life 'in imitation of Christ'. Official canonisation follows a rigid procedure laid down in 1634. Public acclaim often initiates the investigation which starts with an appeal to the Congregation of Rites in Rome, followed by an enquiry which includes a 'Devil's Advocate' arguing against the candidate. Authenticated miracles are often part of the proof offered for the certification of the candidate's worthiness. Then follow three conventions after which, if the Congregation is satisfied, papal consent is given and canonisation takes place in Rome. The new saint is admitted to the Church calendar by the addition of his or her name to an official list and the allocation of a special feast-day.

The first Christians used the term 'saint' for members of the faithful. In time this term came to signify a Christian of outstanding devotion; the earliest saints – the apostles, John the Baptist, the Holy Family and the first martyrs – were acclaimed by common consent. Then, with the evolution of a temporal hierarchy within the church, the bishops became controllers of canonisations within their own diocese. It was not until 1170 that Pope Alexander III insisted that it should be a papal prerogative.

In northern Europe the Reformation brought with it an austerity with a pronounced mistrust of vicarious veneration of the Almighty through gilded statues and graven images. The cult of saints became a prime target for Calvin's iconoclastic beliefs. But the Counter-Reformation of the Catholic Church saw the ever-growing Glorious Company firmly installed as a part of religious belief and practice.

Until the fifteenth century sacred subjects dominated the visual arts; religion was central to cultural development until the Renaissance provided an alternative, Humanist approach. With the Counter-Reformation, devotional paintings and sculpture became increasingly flamboyant as part of anti-Protestant propaganda and inevitably degenerated into predictable artistic platitudes, although individual genius still found expression in the

CONCILIO OECVMENICO VATICANO II INDICTO

IOANNES XXIII

ISTI   LUM

portrayal of sacred subjects. The art of hagiography continued to flourish and in their anxiety to enhance and exalt the virtues of their chosen saint the writers often blurred, and eventually lost sight of, the origins and truths of the lives of the saints.

By the nineteenth century the cult of saints had degenerated into a veneration of pastel-shaded plaster statues and sentimental glorification of saintly sayings and doings. Some respect was restored early in the present century by Pope Pius X who by a papal bull, *Divinu Afflatu*, in 1911 fixed an order of dignity before he himself was canonised. The Virgin Mary has first place, followed by the Holy Angels. Then come St John the Baptist, St Joseph and Sts Peter and Paul. The remaining apostles are next, followed by national and patron

6. The Popes (Maviani) A detail from a conversation piece which includes St Pius X on the left (with halo), who was accredited with miraculous healing before and after his death in 1918.

saints, martyrs, pontiffs, doctors of the church and confessors. Last in the order come virgins and other holy women. In 1969 Pope Paul VI amended the Sanctorial Cycle and demoted certain saints by designating them as local rather than universal.

The lives of the saints reflect a remarkable variety of human dispositions and activities; they are usually benign and always intriguing. The saints in this book – only a small selection from their vast army – are mostly European, since they are inevitably a part of Western heritage and, whether or not we are aware of it, are essential to our folklore and historical tradition.

Apostles and Evangelists

The birth, life and death of Jesus Christ were heralded by the prophecies of John the Baptist and propagated and documented in the tireless preachings and writings of the apostles and evangelists. The most influential of the early Christians have traditionally been accorded special saintly recognition as the eyewitnesses of the living or resurrected Christ and as founders of the early church. They occupy an exalted position. St John the Baptist, the apostles and the evangelists were the most dynamic of these early saints; they interpreted and spread the Messianic message with spectacular results. Essentially, the lives of these New Testament saints were very different from those of the prophets of the Old Testament and their recognisable ordinariness and simplicity made Christian beliefs more accessible to generations of converts.

The birth of John the Baptist, like that of Jesus, was presaged by an angel. He was the child of Elizabeth (a cousin of the Virgin Mary) by her husband Zachary, an old priest. John, a gaunt, compelling figure, emerged from years 'crying in the wilderness' to threaten the local population with impending doom if they did not do penance in preparation for the coming of the Messiah. Unwashed and dressed in a camel skin, John's prophetic appeal attracted a large group of followers, some of whom, rejecting contemporary suspicion of

7. The Beheading of John the Baptist (detail, Puvis de Chavannes) St John was beheaded at the request of Salome, who was eager to have his head on a platter.

'false prophets', later became followers of Christ. The climax of his life's work was his baptism of Christ in the river Jordan, and his words 'Lamb of God who takes away the sins of the world' acknowledged Jesus as the Messiah. John's dramatic imprisonment and execution by the Herod family became a popular legend in Western culture.

The apostles, in their official order, were Simon Peter, Andrew, James the Greater, John, Philip, Bartholomew, Thomas, Matthew, James the Lesser, Jude, Simon the Zealot and Judas Iscariot who was replaced by Matthias. As the acclaimed eyewitnesses of Christ's life and resurrection, they assume the right to represent His teaching. Their first leader, St Peter (originally Simon the Fisherman), epitomised the tortuous experience of self-knowledge through personal failure. From the frightened deserter, who thrice denied his friendship with Christ, he became the beloved pastor who conducted church affairs with conscientiousness and courage. No intellectual, he acquiesced in Paul's doctrines regarding circumcision and diet, which were central to the evolution of Christianity from a Jewish sect into an international religion. Though he may have been superseded as the leader of the Christian church by James of Jerusalem, he continued his apostolic work. Rome, the accepted site of his martyrdom (he was said to have been crucified upside-down at his own request) became the centre of Christendom and now of the Roman Church. Named Peter (The Rock) by Christ, he was an

9. St Peter (wooden statue) St Peter was the first Christian to perform a miracle cure when he made a lame man walk.

8. *Left* **The Martyrdom of Bartholomew** (Ribera)

10. St James the Greater (jet souvenir from Santiago di Compostella) The first apostle to be martyred, James was killed by order of Herod Agrippa in 44AD.

unremarkable but appropriate foundation of the Christian church. His symbol, the crossed keys of heaven, was later adopted by the papacy.

Second only to St Peter was his friend and fellow fisherman St James the Greater, son of Zebedee and brother of St John. Together with Sts Peter and John, he was particularly invited by Christ as a witness to the Agony in the Garden and the Transfiguration. Traditionally James is believed to have travelled to Spain, although there is no substantiated proof of his presence there. Nevertheless, Leo XIII insisted on the authenticity of his relics at Santiago de Compostella. This shrine became one of the most sacred places of medieval pilgrimage. James is usually represented carrying a cockle shell, the pilgrim's emblem.

11. St Andrew (Gaudenzio) He was believed to have been the first Bishop of Byzantium, and so during the Middle Ages his relics were promoted by the Orthodox Church in competition with those of St Peter and Paul in Rome.

St Andrew was St Peter's brother and fellow fisherman. He had been a disciple of John the Baptist and was one of the first apostles to follow Christ. John's gospel is the main source of information about him. St Andrew is venerated in Greece, Scotland and Russia. Another of the first apostles to follow Christ was St Philip, a friend of Sts Peter and Andrew, who, together with the sons of Zebedee, came from the village of Bethsaida. At one time, Philip was sent by Christ as an emissary to represent Him in discussion with the Gentiles.

'What good ever came out of Nazareth?' demanded Nathaniel when asked to meet Jesus, but he, too, was convinced of Christ's divinity at that first meeting. Nathaniel is assumed to be St Bartholomew, the apostle who later preached in Armenia, where he was flayed alive. He is represented carrying a butcher's knife or occasionally his own skin. Christ described him as 'an Israelite, indeed, in whom there is no guile'.

'Doubting' Thomas rejected the reality of Christ's resurrection until invited to touch Christ's wounds, which abruptly restored his faith. Thomas is often depicted at this moment of confrontation with the Risen Christ and this incident has always been used by the church as an example of the necessity of faith in the seemingly impossible. He was adopted by the Malabar Indians as their apostolic founder, as he was reputed to have lived among them as a carpenter-preacher and to have been martyred in India. Thomas is the patron saint of architects, masons and stone-cutters.

St James the Lesser was the son of Alphaeus and the brother of St Jude. He may have been related either to St Joseph or to the Virgin Mary. He is also said to have been James of Jerusalem, 'the Lord's brother', who assumed leadership of the Christian community in Jerusalem from St Peter. James was either stoned to death or thrown from the pinnacle of the temple of Jerusalem but, having survived miraculously, he was finally clubbed to death and a club became his symbol. His protracted death is representative of the early Christian martyrs' ability to perform miracles of self-preservation, ascribed to divine intervention.

His brother, St Jude, was also known as Thaddaeus. It is held that he preached in Mesopotamia and was martyred there with St Simon the Zealot. He often appears carrying a halberd and is the patron of 'those in desperate straits'. The cult of St Jude is still strongly supported by those seeking intercession for lost causes.

St Simon the Zealot was probably a member of the Zealots, a group of Jewish religious extremists. He was sawn in half in Persia and is therefore represented holding a saw, or a book, demonstrating his zeal for Mosaic law.

After the betrayal of Christ by Judas Iscariot, the first Christian to commit suicide, St Matthias became the twelfth apostle. He is a shadowy figure about whom little is known.

Sts Matthew and John were not only numbered among the twelve apostles but were also evangelists who, with Sts Mark and Luke, wrote the four gospels. Both these activities were fundamental to the development of the Christian religion. Matthew contributed the first gospel, 'the Gift of Yaweh', which was initially the most influential in church practice and is now considered the great ecclesiastical gospel. Not much is known of him personally. Matthew was called by Christ from his post as a tax collector for the Romans at Capernaum and, after his life as a disciple, he is supposed to have been martyred in Ethiopia or Persia. His gospel was written in Aramaic, principally for the Jews, and was contemporary with those of Luke and Mark (50–63 AD), which three are known as the synoptic gospels.

St Mark was a disciple of the first Christian community in Jerusalem and a close friend of St

12. St Matthew (Book of Kells) Portrayed here as an evangelist, Matthew was often shown with a sword or halberd, or in his role as tax collector.

Peter. The basis of his gospel derived from Peter's testimony. Written in Greek, his is the second canonical gospel and it interprets and explains Jewish rites and geography to non-Jews. Mark was the first bishop of Alexandria, where he was martyred, having alarmed the authorities by a miracle-cure of a

13. The Miracle of St Mark (Tintoretto) St Mark is depicted here intervening to rescue a slave from bondage.

local shoemaker. Mark's emblem is a winged lion, still ubiquitous in Venice, where he is the patron saint and whose citizens venerate his relics.

The third evangelist, St Luke, was a medical

16

14. Sts Mark and Luke (Chiaroscuro woodcut after Lallemand) The two evangelists sharing the symbol of the book (The Gospel).

man and a painter. Although he had not been an eyewitness to the events of Christ's life, his gospel is the most admired for its vivid account of the essentially human aspect of Jesus' personality. Luke accompanied St Paul on some of his missions and on his final journey to Rome. He is reputed to have lived to the age of eighty-four and to have died in Greece.

The last and most extraordinary of the evangelists was the apostle St John, 'beloved of

15. St Paul Commanding St Luke to Accompany Him on the Missionary Journeys to Rome (de la Fosse) St Luke was St Paul's companion during his last days before his execution in Rome.

Christ' and the only member of the apostolic group not to desert Him at the Crucifixion. John is described in the gospels as a gentle person but, paradoxically, he and his brother, James, were named 'the sons of thunder' by Christ after an incident with inhospitable Samaritan villagers, when the brothers threatened to 'ask the Lord to bring down fire and consume them'. John witnessed the founding of the church and the Diaspora. His gospel was written as a metaphysical and symbolic interpretation of the story of Jesus (after the other three had already established it as the Message), which became the foundation of Christian philosophy. It is known that John was exiled on the island of Patmos in later life and he may have written his gospel there. Later he retired to Ephesus, where he preached fervently of Christian love. Two legends of miraculous survival attach to St John: one in which he emerged unharmed from immersion in boiling oil by the Romans and another in which he escaped death from a poisoned cup, when it was transformed into a snake which fled. This 'Cup of Charity' was commemorated by a European feast-day. By whatever means he finally expired, he is known to have died an old man. St John's emblem is an eagle, symbolic of the majestic heights of his gospel prologue. As the attributed author of the Apocalypse,

16. Jesus and the Apostles (contemporary puzzle)

he is considered to be the first Christian mystic.

St Paul is regarded as the single most important figure in Christian history apart from Christ himself. He was the architect of Christian theology and the apostle of the Gentiles. Described as small, bald, bearded and bandy-legged Paul (at that time known as Saul) was a troubled student of theology, who became a Pharisee notorious for ferreting out Christians during their persecution by the Romans. The familiar story of his dramatic conversion on the road to Damascus is characteristic of Paul's consistent ability to interpret events as symbolic and act on them accordingly. This interpretative power enabled him to view Christ's life and death as universally significant, as well as a part of the Jewish faith. Combining this idea with an absolute belief in the Salvation of Christ, Paul travelled continuously for thirty years, communicating the Message to the world. Paul was the ablest of the first missionaries and his ardent commitment and dedication were remarkable. His energy was phenomenal, complemented by his dominating personality which is still evident today in his writings. He gave the formative church a formal intellectual framework, demonstrated again in his prolific letters, in which his own perplexities became the problems of new religious thinking. Paul is set apart from the apostles in that he had no personal acquaintance with Christ. After his conversion, he was able to contribute more ardently, perhaps, than any of them and therefore his doctrines and writings are the more convincing to the unconverted.

These first saints were essential to the sure foundation and rapid expansion of Christianity. The leadership of St Peter, the doctrines and writings of St Paul, the illuminating gospels of the evangelists and the energy of the peripatetic apostles were the cornerstones of what became the most powerful institution in the Western world – the Christian church.

17. St Sebastian
(contemporary Brazilian
plaster statue) Because he
was ultimately immunised
against the arrows,
Sebastian is invoked
against contagious
diseases.

Martyrs

Fear of pain is common to us all. The idea of suffering agonies for an ideal is as challenging as it is horrifying.

A coveted Christian goal during the formative years of the church was to die a martyr's death. Martyrdom was believed to ensure the victim's place in heaven by 'baptism of fire', emphasising the unimportance of earthly life in the face of the apocalypse, then considered imminent. These beliefs created the motive and were then reinforced by the veneration accorded those who were martyred.

By the reign of the Emperor Nero, Christian persecutions had reached a frenzied pitch. The initial reasons for them were the Christians' refusal to profess allegiance to the official Roman religion and their behaviour as an outlawed proselytising sect who practised secret rites, which were believed to involve a form of cannibalism. As the most spectacular of the early Christian saintly cults, martyrdom produced heroic victims, sung and unsung, by the thousands.

The first official Christian martyr was St Stephen, a Hellenised Jew with a reputation as a zealous preacher. He was one of the first seven deacons, blessed by the apostles, who were the nucleus of the new church. On trial for blasphemy, Stephen denounced the Jewish council in Jerusalem as the murderers of Christ, as their ancestors had murdered the prophets. Stephen also called them 'stiff-necked people uncircumcised in heart and ears' and after a further diatribe he was condemned, dragged outside the city walls and stoned to death. Stephen's martyrdom is a verifiable historical fact and Saul, later known as Paul, witnessed his execution.

The cults of his successors, often mythical anyway, are characterised by supernatural occurrences of repeated quasi-divine phenomena. A typical example was St Sebastian, a Roman soldier, martyred during the rule of the Emperor Diocletian. His existence is questionable, but the story goes that he was a holy and dedicated worker for the Christian cause, denounced by a false disciple and condemned to be shot to death with arrows. He was left for dead after his execution, but during the night he was cured by the widow of another martyr. Reappearing the very next day before Diocletian, Sebastian reproached him, and the former, not surprisingly, had him clubbed to death. Known as 'the holy pincushion' and a favourite male nude during later periods when religious subject matter still dominated the visual arts, St Sebastian is the patron of archers, soldiers and those stricken with plague.

Another legendary figure who was exceptionally popular was St George, the champion of princesses and slayer of dragons. The story of his heroic rescue of a nubile princess from the slavering jaws of a monstrous dragon, by piercing it with his trusty lance, inspired the church to substitute his April feast-day for the old pagan spring rites. St George is the patron of soldiers and Boy Scouts and

18. St Sebastian (Honhorst) A painting which shows him as the perfect victim, before his miraculous cure.

19. *Above right* **St George and the Dragon** (Italian postage stamps)

20. St George and the Dragon (Coptic manuscript) As the Christian adaptation of the spring festival, the Orthodox rites for his feast day included couples rolling on the ground to promote a good harvest.

of England, Portugal, Catalonia, Genoa and Venice. He was also venerated in the East, where he was known as Megalomartyros.

One famous Roman martyr who actually existed was St Lawrence. He was clearly an attractive character with a sense of humour, rare in victims. He was a deacon of Rome who, it is said, when asked to hand over the church treasure to the city prefect, gathered a motley bunch of paupers and invalids together and presented them to the official, saying, 'Here is the church's treasure.' Although decapitation was then the current form of execution, Lawrence was roasted to death on a gridiron and while he was roasting politely suggested that he be rotated on the spit so that the result should be evenly cooked. In Rome five early basilicas were dedicated to St Lawrence, as is the Escorial in Spain, and in the seventh century his relics were a papal gift to the King of Northumbria.

Sts Cosmas and Damian were mysterious figures. Supposedly brothers, who used their skills as physicians without payment for the benefit of the poor, they were said to have performed numerous miraculous cures. The most famous of these was the transplant of a black's leg onto the body of a sleeping white, who woke up to find that he had a mismatched pair of legs. Their deaths were similarly spectacular; thrown into the raging sea, they were rescued by an angel, after which they were bound to crosses and stoned, but the rocks boomeranged and killed their tormentors. Finally they were successfully beheaded. Their deaths probably occurred at Cyrrhus in Syria, but their cult had spread throughout the Christian world by the fifth century; they became the patrons of doctors and people would sleep in churches dedicated to them in the hope that they would be blessedly cured.

A substantial figure was St Denis, also known as St Dionysus, who was sent to Gaul as a missionary during the third century and was martyred at Mont-

21. The Death of St Peter Martyr (Bernardino) Ambushed and
killed on his way to Milan, the Dominican preacher was said to have
written the words 'Credo in Deum' in his own blood as he died.

22. St Lawrence Preparing for Martyrdom (Elseheimer) Although he refused to relinquish the church's funds to the Roman Prefecture, Lawrence was a symbol of the church's disinterest in material things.

28

23. The Miracle of Sts Cosmas and Damian (Fra Angelico) The brothers are invoked as aids to those in need of medical treatment.

martre in Paris, three years later. Wonderful legends grew up around his death. St Denis was said to have been a cephalophore, a head carrier, and to have carried his severed head to his grave. He was also reputed to have grown as many as seven heads in the manner of Osiris, whose limbs multiplied after he had been dismembered and buried. St Denis is the patron saint of Paris and the popular patron of

France, as he converted many Gauls when he preached on an island in the Seine.

Another famous legend grew up around St Eustace, who was a Roman general called Placidus. While out hunting, he encountered a stag with a luminous crucifix between its antlers. Recognising this as a supernatural sign, Placidus converted, which disgraced him and lost him his family and fortune. He was forced to become an agricultural labourer and called himself Eustace. But the threat of a barbarian invasion impelled the Emperor Trajan to reinstate him as the general of the defending army. On returning home triumphant to be reunited with his family, Eustace was required to make an official thanksgiving sacrifice to the gods. This he refused to do, so Trajan, furious with his unpatriotic attitude, ordered that he, with his wife and children, be thrown to the lions. However, 'instead of harming these faithful servants of God, the beasts merely frisked and frolicked about them'. Increased imperial rage followed and the wretched family was locked inside a bronze bull in which they were roasted to death. St Eustace is the patron of hunters.

At the beginning of the second century a fiery bishop, St Ignatius of Antioch, was condemned to be thrown to the wild beasts at the amphitheatre in Rome. Although treated with respect by the Roman authorities (he was allowed to visit favoured Christian communities on his way to Rome) St Ignatius, determined on a martyr's death, declared that even if the beasts were not hungry he would urge them to devour him. He was not disappointed as the wild beasts left nothing of his body except a few bones, which were taken to Antioch but eventually returned to Rome where they were enshrined in the church of St Clement. Ignatius described himself as the 'wheat of Christ', a term of strong eucharistic parallels. The association between Christ as the sacrificial victim (regenerated through the ceremony of the eucharist and through transubstantiation) and the martyrs offering themselves in his memory displays a prime element of Christian martyrdom.

Another example, that of St Polycarp, illustrates further their motivation. St Polycarp was the bishop of Smyrna, also in Syria, and a contemporary of St Ignatius. He bravely refused to worship the official gods and to curse Christ, saying, 'I have served him eighty-six years and he has done me no wrong; how can I blaspheme the King who has preserved me?' On hearing that he was to be burnt to death, he replied that the fire of one hour could not compare with the fires of eternal punishment. When the flames had been kindled, Polycarp's body was described as looking 'not like burning flesh, but like the bread in the oven . . . or gold and silver being refined in a furnace'. The official account of his death, written by witnesses who collected his bones, stated that he was first killed by a sword and then burnt.

The craving of St Ignatius to be eaten by wild beasts and his passionate veneration of the eucharist ('the medicine of immortality and antidote of death') and the description of Polycarp's 'breadlike' body point up the function of the martyr cult to sustain the nostalgia of Christ's death. The martyrs' belief in the glories of afterlife continue the celebration of Christ's resurrection as an essential Christian experience. The cults of personal examples of horrific sacrifice existed as reminders of humanity's responsibility for the Crucifixion. Christ's death is unique in that it can never really be mourned; his resurrection put a stop to that. Perhaps if mourning is an acceptance of loss and is essential to the celebration of new life, then Christians have always been denied this emotional release and thus guilt is notionally retained within the religious code. Ordinary beings are perpetually humbled by the glowing examples of the martyrs.

24. The Vision of St Eustace (Pisanello) The crucified Christ
appeared to St Eustace between a deer's antlers.

31

25. The Martyrdom of Catherine (Orsi) The patroness of philosophers, apologists and wainwrights, St Catherine was tied to an elaborate wheel which was shattered by divine intervention.

Virgin Martyrs

The word 'martyr' is exotic and the word 'virgin' is titillating. Compounded, they illustrate the inherent roles of sex and violence typical of the virgin martyrs of the Christian tradition.

Celibacy was encouraged during the persecutions of the early Christian church, for practical reasons to sustain a militant underground, but the origins of the cult of virgin martyrs predate these considerations. The Hellenic philosophers relegated women to an inferior status in most things and the Jews characterised Eve, the first woman, as a lethal temptress. As St Jerome confirmed in his time, 'Virginity is natural and marriage came after the fall.' The same historical prejudice is epitomised in Ecclesiasticus XXV, 24:

'Woman is the origin of all sin
and it is through her that we all die.'

This, and similar dire warnings, promoted the Christian concept of sexual abstinence as synonymous with virtue, and virginity, as proof of such abstinence, accordingly denoted virtue.

Thus a body of thought emerged which denied women's natural desires and yet blamed them for their necessarily devious powers of seduction. Christian women were educated to believe that to 'lose' their virginity would render them essentially incomplete; they and their partners would be spiritually damaged by the memory of an association, however brief, which might demand a human intimacy, as substitute for total commitment to God. To emphasise this belief, veneration of the virgin martyrs was encouraged and the virgin saints were prominently positioned in the holy hierarchy.

In the manner of romantic fiction, the legends of the virgins centre on a heroine who is beautiful, intelligent and good. Innocently provoking lust in her persecutor, she is ultimately martyred by torture and eventual death. Christian tenets provide the moral armour to cling to a faith which is reaffirmed by an horrific martyrdom which, in itself, expunges the original guilt of having been the cause of lust.

The earliest story of a virgin martyr grew up around St Catherine of Alexandria. Although there is no solid proof of her existence, veneration of Catherine began in the early years of Christianity. St Catherine was a girl of outstanding beauty and high intelligence who attracted the attention of the Roman Emperor Maxentius by protesting against idol-worship (having defended her beliefs so ably that she confounded fifty of the Emperor's philosophers in theological debate). Maxentius proposed marriage: she refused and was then beaten for two hours, imprisoned, and tied to a spiked 'Catherine' wheel. The wheel miraculously shattered and the two hundred watching soldiers were promptly converted. In frustrated rage, Maxentius had them all beheaded along with Catherine, from whose severed arteries flowed milk. Since pre-Christian times, milk has always been a metaphysical symbol of fertility, nutrition and healing. It emerges in the image of the Virgin Mary suckling the Christ-child, in the concept of a 'land flowing with milk and honey', and in expressions such as 'veins flowing with the milk of human kindness'. In the middle ages St Catherine was revered as a mystical bride of Christ, confirming the notion (in imitation of the Virgin Mary) of a virgin's 'marriage' to God. In recognition of this relationship, nuns often wear wedding rings on their right hands.

St Margaret, patroness of childbirth, whose legend spread from the East during the Crusades, was supposedly the daughter of a pagan priest of Antioch at the time of Diocletian. Secretly converted to Christianity by her nurse, she rejected advances made to her by the prefect Olibrius, who denounced her as a Christian. She was then tortured so horribly that Olibrius himself could not bear to watch her agonies. While in prison, she was visited by the devil in the form of a monster who, with his hideous and inflamed maw agape, sought to terrify and confound her; he fled, vampire-like before a cross with which she confronted him. Despite the menaces of this Freudian beast, Margaret managed to convert as many as five hundred people each day, which so infuriated Olibrius that he had her beheaded.

St Barbara has been a considerable figure since the ninth century, although it is not known precisely when or where the events of her martyrdom took place. A beautiful girl, she was locked in a tower by her father, Dioscurus, to discourage her numerous suitors. There she was secretly converted to Christianity, but Dioscurus, on discovering this, denounced her to the authorities who tortured her and ordered Dioscurus to kill her. In so doing, Dioscurus was struck by lightning and reduced to a cinder. Consequently St Barbara is invoked against death, thunder, lightning and gunpowder and has become the patron saint of gunners and miners.

Unlike the latter three legends, the evidence for the story of St Ursula is more substantial. At

26. St Barbara (oak figure) St Barbara with her tower, which symbolises her powers as the protectress of those dying without the sacraments.

Cologne, a church rebuilt on the site of the martyrdom of a group of virgins contains an inscribed stone which provides proof of St Ursula's probable existence, but the legend surrounding her martyrdom is fantastic. St Ursula, the daughter of an English king, stipulated that her suitor, if he truly wished to marry her, must collect together ten thousand virgins and ships to carry them with her on a pilgrimage. The suitor complied and Ursula set off and arrived in Cologne after extensive travels (which, in some versions of the story, included Rome, where the pilgrimage was joined by the admiring Pope). But at Cologne an invading horde of

27. The Dream of St Ursula (Carpaccio)

30. The Martyrdom of St Julitta (Catalan painting) A Spanish noblewoman, St Julitta was sawn in half for her refusal to deny her Christian beliefs.

29. *Left* **St Lucy** (Crivelli) A beautiful Sicilian virgin, St Lucy was martyred at Syracuse. After being wooed by a lascivious suitor, she plucked out her eyes and sent them to him on a plate. She is invoked against diseases of the eye.

28. *Facing page* **The Martyrdom of Ursula and her Maidens** (Memling) She is the patroness of female education.

Huns became outraged at the sight of all these potential Christian mothers and this was aggravated by Ursula's rebuttal of their leader's advances. Ursula exhorted her maidens to be killed rather than submit to sexual abuse from their tormentors, offering herself as the first victim as an example to the others, all of whom were massacred. St Ursula is the patron saint of young girls and their instructresses.

One of the greatest patron saints was the Roman virgin martyr, St Cecilia, whose cult has been extremely popular since the sixth century. An account of her martyrdom had been written by 545 but, like certain of the relics associated with her, is probably not genuine. Cecilia was a young and lovely Roman noblewoman who, as a Christian, had consecrated her virginity to God. On her wedding day she told her husband, Valerian, of her vow and he, impressed by her resolve, not only respected her wishes, but himself converted, as did his brother, Tiburtius. Both brothers were arrested and executed. Cecilia was interrogated by the prefect and condemned to death for refusing to worship idols. At first, she was sentenced to be steamed to death in her bathroom, but after a day and a night 'the flames had no power over her body, neither was a hair of her head singed'. After an officer, who had been issued with orders to behead her, struck the fatal blows, Cecilia lay for two days and nights beside her bath with her head half-severed before she finally expired. In the sixteenth century, Cecilia was adopted as the patroness of musicians, for she was said to have sung to the Lord in her heart during her marriage ceremony. She is often represented playing the organ.

Another significant Roman virgin was St Agnes, whose remains in the church dedicated to her in Rome's Piazza Navona might be genuine, but whose story has become obscured by legends. As a girl of twelve or thirteen, she was ordered to obey

31. St Cecilia (terracotta bust, attrib. Donatello) As the patroness of musicians, her feast-day is marked by concerts and special anthems.

Diocletian's rigid law compelling Christians to offer incense at the altar of Minerva. Agnes refused to do so and was publicly humiliated (at the site of the present church) by being stripped in full view of the watching crowd. A young man, who dared to look at her profanely, fell convulsed to the ground, whereupon Agnes' hair tumbled down, miraculously covering her nakedness. She was then stabbed in the throat and thus qualified for her martyr's

32. St Agnes (Ribera) Martyred at the age of thirteen, St Agnes is the protectress of teenagers.

marriage for her with the King of Sicily, little knowing that Wilgefortis had taken a vow of chastity. She prayed for deliverance and her faith was amply rewarded with a beard, which grew overnight and repelled her prospective husband. Her father was so angry that he had her crucified.

Variations on the theme include the legend of St Uncumber, who was invoked by English women against tiresome husbands, and the Irish St Brigid, whose beauty was transformed to ugliness to thwart

33. St Wilgefortis (detail, Memling) with the miraculous, if wispy, beard which grew to protect her virtue.

palm. Her emblem is a sacrificial lamb.

The theme of women being instantly covered and protected by their hair recurs in the story of Lady Godiva, who was publicly shamed by being forced to ride naked through the streets of Coventry. It is also illustrated in more extreme form, when virgins have sprouted beards to defend their virtue.

One such tale is the legend of St Wilgefortis, the daughter of a Portuguese king, who arranged a

her suitors. Her looks were restored to their former loveliness once safe in the haven of a convent.

St Agatha was the great virgin martyr of Sicily. She was an exquisite young noblewoman from Catania, desired by the consul Quintian. When Agatha repulsed his advances he ordered her breasts to be torn off. The night after this ordeal, St Peter appeared to her and healed her wounds. The next day she was killed by being rolled naked upon

34. St Agatha (Zurburan) Sicilians living near Mt Etna invoke St Agatha to protect them against the rages of the volcano.

35. Maria Goretti is upheld in Catholic schools as the perfect example of Christian girlhood.

potsherds. St Agatha is the patroness of bell-founders because bells are breast-shaped: round loaves used to be blessed on her feast-day in celebration of her suffering.

Such gruesome tales, which have served as foundations of many cults throughout Christian history, cannot be merely considered as a colourful, if repetitive, series of legends. One modern example of the force of this tradition lies in the circumstances of the death and canonisation of St Maria Goretti.

Maria was a beautiful and deeply religious Italian peasant who had dedicated herself to God. In 1902, at the age of twelve, she consistently resisted the advances of a youth who soon threatened to kill her. Even though he terrified her and tormented her with the knife which he intended to use, Maria would not surrender and he stabbed her fatally. Surviving until the following day, she willingly forgave her murderer on her deathbed. Her bravery resulted in her canonisation in 1950, as a 'Victim of Holy Purity'.

36. Pope Paul VI visiting the shrine of Maria Goretti at Nettuno.

Maria's religious conditioning preferred death to violation. 'People like Maria Goretti . . . have an ever present realisation that lightly to surrender one's bodily integrity, even to the most compelling needs of the moment, upsets the whole rhythm of the universe. Perhaps this is the chief reason why the canonisation of Maria Goretti at the height of the splendours of the last Holy Year strikes one as being particularly significant and timely. It came as a clarion call of protest against the hopeless dreariness of base personal standards: the saint was canonised for our benefit, not for hers.' (From *The Saints*, A Concise Biographical Dictionary, edited by John Coulson, The Caxton Publishing Company Ltd, 1958.) The Catholic Church instead of mourning her murder used it to reaffirm an archaic belief that the sanctity of human life should be subordinate to the guilt of sexual experience; the guilt is successfully transferred to the victim who is redeemed only through martyrdom or penance. The acceptance of this concept continues a cult which is as curious as it is primitive.

37. The Conversion of St Paul on the Road to Damascus (Caravaggio)

Theologians

Unfortunately for the Christian theologians their saviour was neither the Judaic Yaweh nor the Platonic idea of the eternal deity, but something between the two. His hybrid identity was first defined by St Paul, who related his idea of his God to his idea of mankind at length and with great detail. The Jesus Christ of the scriptures was transformed from the Son of Yaweh into a part of a universal deity who suffered from an acute case of multiple personality. This prompted a natural need for further questions and answers in godfearing Christians, which kept the scientists of religion in business explaining the nature of the Christian God and the Christian faith for the next two thousand years. Just as the earthly nature of Christ and the friendly company of saints created a more approachable atmosphere in which to worship an awesome God, so the theologians brought a reassuring order to the undeniable chaos arising from individual interpretations of God.

The ardent language of the scriptures could be explained symbolically and presented to the faithful scientifically but, as beliefs cannot always be reduced to a logical formula, the theologians found themselves wrestling with solutions and problems eternally baffling in their intrinsic contradictions. They became central to Christian thinking.

In the same direct manner as the literal explanation of his dramatic conversion on the road to Damascus, St Paul perceived Christ's ministry, death and resurrection as the revelation of His role as the lawgiver and saviour of mankind. Paul chose to see man as naturally corrupt and therefore unable to save his own soul without the benefit of Christ's mercy. He refined the concept of the Christian need to gain spiritual salvation with the idea that 'only some' are saved. St Paul's energy and personality ensured that his beliefs were widely heard and understood through his tireless missionary work and his ideas are still argued and reinterpreted today. Through Paul's work alone, Christian theology was based on an immediate and powerful controversy.

By the fourth century Christianity was the favoured religion of the Western Roman Empire and as it pervaded a variety of cultures and encountered alternative beliefs it started to fragment. Central to this fragmentation was the Arian heresy which created the great ideological split within the Christian religion before the Reformation. Arianism was based on the concept of the unity of the Trinity, refuting Christ's right to its membership and claiming that he was made by God and therefore a mortal creature, albeit an exceptionally special and holy one. This theory threatened the carefully preserved and difficult orthodoxy of Christian doctrine, moving yet further away from the classical Greek concept of unity, but a group of theologians known as the Greek doctors or fathers of the church eventually refuted it successfully through their voluble writings and arguments. They became honoured as the guardians of Christian ideology and therefore very special saints.

In 325 the first ecumenical council of the Christian church, held at Nicaea, condemned the teaching of Arias. This was mainly due to the work of a squat Egyptian called Athanasius who became the Bishop of Alexandria. Later, Arianism was restored to favour and Athanasius spent many years in exile but, even from the deserts of Upper Egypt. he had sufficient personality and zeal to attract a faithful following. He declared that the incarnation of God in Christ was proof that divinity and humanity are not mutually exclusive and thus the idea grew of the consubstantiality of the Trinity. Perplexing and amazing as these beliefs sound they were the burning questions of the day, propounded publicly just as politics are today. Athanasius, who declared his views in the controversy at the expense of personal comfort, was admired and then venerated as an heroic theologian.

The turbulent bitterness with which Arianism was defended and opposed can be seen clearly in the lives of two other Greek doctors, Sts Gregory of Nazianzus and Basil of Caesarea. Gregory of Nazianzus was the son of the Bishop of Cappadocia (celibacy was not yet a strict condition of priesthood) and members of his family were distinguished theologians in the church establishment. After studying at the University of Athens, where he befriended St Basil of Caesarea, he joined him as a solitary in Pontus where he planned to spend his life as a monk. But after two years he returned home to help his aged father and was, very unwillingly, ordained. He ran away to rejoin Basil but soon felt bound to return home again where he wrote an apologia for his behaviour which came to be considered a classic definition of the nature and function of the priesthood. Known to be a shy and sensitive man, he was ineluctably drawn into public life by his growing oratorical reputation and writing skills and thus Gregory was eventually positioned in the forefront of theological politics.

In 381, at the General Council of Constantinople, Gregory was appointed Bishop of Constantinople and gave five discourses on the doctrine of the Trinity as instituted fifty years previously. Because of his anti-Arian stance he was attacked by the Arian groups both physically and verbally. The continued hostility aged him prematurely and at fifty-five he retired to his estates to spend his final years writing and contemplating. After his death Gregory became universally venerated and his relics rested at Constantinople before being translated to St Peter's in Rome.

St Basil of Caesarea had a similar background and early career to Gregory but, after five years at Pontus, he set down a series of principles which were the foundation of the Rule of Eastern monasticism. He was then appointed Bishop of Caesarea where he was persecuted by the Emperor Valens who was a convinced Arian. Basil's hot-blooded temperament and his tactlessness thrust him into the centre of ideological disputes. Well-known for his championship of the under-privileged and intolerance of the excesses of the ruling classes, his writings, sermons and letters show a commitment and are outspoken. They comprehend doctrines of a broader nature than those which concerned his contemporaries. He has been honoured as a formidable fighter in the cause of orthodoxy, evident in his legislation of his monastic Rule, and his name is still invoked frequently in the Eastern church today.

The fourth of the Greek doctors in the tradition of battling theologians was St John Chrysostom, known as the 'Golden Mouth'. A native of Antioch, who after an education in oratory and law spent eight years in a damp cave in the mountains near his birthplace, John became a priest and soon waded into the heart of church politics. By the end of the fourth century he was consecrated Archbishop of Constantinople and for the remaining nine years of his life fought the decadence and corrup-

38. St Basil (Herrera) A theologian and monastic innovator, Basil was the son, grandson and brother of saints.

39. St John Chrysostom
(Lampardos) Described as
small, spidery, pale and
bald, John became the
patron of preachers.

46

tion of the Byzantine see. His main adversary was the Empress Eudoxia whose influence was threatened by John's criticisms of the imperial court. Undeterred by her vicious opposition, John continued to reform the Rules of the clergy until banished by Eudoxia; frightened by a severe earthquake which shook Constantinople she recalled him, only to exile him again as soon the tremors and her terror had subsided. John died in exile but his body was returned to Constantinople thirty years later. His reputation as a theologian rests mainly on his clear interpretation of the testaments, church history and the work of St Paul and on his gift of direct communication which was a startling and welcome innovation in an age of convoluted politics and ideological conundrums.

Four other theologians esteemed as guardians of Christian doctrine were known as the Latin doctors. The first of them, St Ambrose, was a Latin doctor in the same style as his Greek contemporaries – a fiery political fighter whose preoccupation was defining the nature of his God; that is, his belief. Ambrose was the Governor of Amelia and Liguria and in 374 he was elected Bishop of Milan and was baptised, ordained and consecrated Bishop of the administrative centre of the Western Roman Empire. He insisted that the power of the church should not be subject to imperial interference. He humbled the Emperor Theodosius by making him do public penance for the brutal massacre of thousands of his subjects in retaliation for the murder of the governor in Thessalonika. On another occasion when he had refused to hand over one of his Milanese churches for the use of the Arians he was besieged by the Empress' followers but steadfastly refused to permit them entry. By such bold acts and oratory Ambrose persuaded his contemporaries in the Western church that they could not entertain Arian

40. St Ambrose (Pacher) His emblem is a beehive.

principles and remain true to the original Christian doctrines.

His eloquence was responsible for the conversion of the younger distinguished scholar, St Augustine of Hippo, who was not baptised but was educated as a Christian before he studied rhetoric and Platonic philosophy. He was then briefly a sceptic and later he spent nine years studying Manichaeism, a school of thought representing

41. St Augustine with the Holy Family and St Catherine of Alexandria (Garofalo) Catherine is acting as muse and giving heavenly encouragement to Augustine, the reformed rake.

Satan as coeternal with God and predicated on the division of the universe into two warring groups; the Spirit (of God) and the Flesh (of Satan). Before his eventual conversion Augustine was inclined to the victory of the Flesh but, renouncing his earlier beliefs, he was made Bishop of Hippo and established a monastic community whose Rule is still employed today by the Augustinian friars. During this time he wrote prolifically; his most famous works were his *Confessions*, an autobiography, and *The City of God*, the first Christian philosophical history. Augustine was then the most influential Christian theologian since St Paul. He combined the discipline and range of an extensive education, both formal and personally-directed, with powerful and original persuasiveness. Like St Paul he was obsessed with his own life and conversion which coloured his view of human beings, whom he regarded as sinful and inadequate and thus in desperate need of salvation through divine grace and mercy. Augustine's arrogance arose from his understandable appreciation of his own intellect and effectiveness. It was displayed by his publicly proclaiming his repentance and his means of finding personal salvation as pertinent to all. He publicly absolved himself. This joyless approach and belief in the necessity for religion as the sole means of achieving salvation, rendered essential by man's original sin, dwelt on penance and punishment. Augustine was a Christian thinker who by force of a considerable personality presented his own views as pertinent to universal enlightenment. His guilt became exemplified as mankind's guilt: a Christian heritage which lingers today.

Another professed sinner, who busied himself detecting sin in his fellows, was the supreme biblical scholar, Eusebius Hieronymous, called St Jerome. Famous for his temper and penitential efforts, Jerome spent most of his life in solitude in imitation of the desert fathers. He was the harbinger of monkish scholarship, a linguist of distinction and the transla-

tor of what became the standard Latin version of the Bible, the Vulgate, still used by the Roman Catholic Church today. His other project was the study of monasticism in which he demonstrated his pre-occupation with the issue of celibacy which perplexed him. He wrote at length about chastity, so

42. The Penitent Jerome (detail, da Vinci)

fervently so that he warned husbands that 'he who too ardently loves his wife is an adulterer'. Jerome's life was typical of those reclusive individuals who also enjoyed participating in religious politics like Sts Bernard, Bruno, Catherine of Siena, Basil of Caesarea and Gregory of Nazianzus, who was Jerome's teacher. When he was not a practising solitary Jerome made enemies easily; his hideous temper became renowned and his pomposity irritated his peers. Even a thousand years later his tarnished reputation prompted Pope Sixtus V, on viewing a painting of St Jerome furiously beating his breast with a stone, to say, 'You do well to use that stone;

without it you would never have been numbered among the saints.' Nevertheless his scholarship was undeniable and for this he is honoured as one of the four Latin doctors. Both Augustine and Jerome were preoccupied with defining the nature of sin; that is, the need for their belief.

43. St Jerome in his Study (Catena) After his time as a solitary, St Jerome became secretary to Pope St Damascus. The lion which often accompanies him in paintings became his bodyguard after he removed a thorn from its paw.

At the end of the sixth century the Roman church was ruled by one of its most remarkable popes, Gregory the Great, last of the Latin doctors.

44. St Gregory (Goya) Gregory was said to be always writing; Europe was thick with messengers carrying letters of instruction to his clergy, covering every area of church practice.

thirteen years of his papal reign he established the papacy as the great temporal power of the middle ages. He organised a legal system based on Roman and Christian legal principles. His reign survived invasions, floods and famines, and he despatched missionary expeditions (one of which was St Augustine of Canterbury's to the English) and wrote prodigiously about most aspects of church practice and Christian doctrine. Gregory's writings influenced Christian thinking for hundreds of years as well as establishing his own reputation as one of the most effective popes in history. His writings interpreted the intricacies of the theological and cultural cross-pollination of the earlier church fathers with the converted barbarians, who were to become the new faithful, and consolidated his policy of steering the church toward the West and away from Byzantine rivalry. His grasp of legal problems resulted in his view on the functions of the episcopate becoming standard practice and his imaginative *Lives of the Saints* authenticated the ever-growing preoccupation with the miraculous which flourished during the middle ages. His theological importance was in his application of established ideas adapted to meet new needs arising from the evolution of Christianity. He applied his belief to temporal needs. Gregory was a ruler, sure of his power, but careful to style himself 'the servant of the servants of God', a title still used by popes today.

Through the work of St Paul and its interpretation by the eight great doctors Christian theology gradually developed into a complex and homogeneous body of thought which remained substantially unchanged until the thirteenth century when it was reconstructed through the classical, systematic arguments of St Thomas Aquinas, the Dominican theologian.

Thomas' intention to become a mendicant friar shocked his family who tried to dissuade him

A Roman patrician monk, St Gregory's interest originally lay in the monastic 'heresy' as the most lasting form of organised Christianity. During the

by locking him in the family fortress at Rocca Secca for a year. Not to be deterred, he joined the Dominicans at the age of nineteen and went to Paris to study under Albert Magnus. Thomas became bald when still young and grew enormously fat. He was reputed to have had a crescent carved out of his dining table to accommodate his vast belly. He had remarkable powers of concentration and at times would dictate to four secretaries simultaneously. His life was spent lecturing, studying, writing and commuting between Paris and Italy until he died of exhaustion at the age of forty-nine. Thomas' work was the summit of intellectual achievement in the middle ages. He studied Arabic, Judaic, classical and Christian texts and then fused them, using Aristotelian casuistry, into a comprehensive orderly exposition of theology. His scientific approach defined reason and faith as separate and complementary elements: reason aids the understanding of belief and faith starts where reason reaches its limits. Belief in truths attained by reasonable argument is compatible with beliefs realised through 'the divine rationale'. The clarity and logic of his argument is still recognised and Aquinas' major work, *Summa Theologica*, although unfinished, became a standard theological text. He was canonised within fifty years of his death and is venerated as the 'doctor communis' or universal teacher.

In spite of the difficulties of arguing around a monotheistic concept centuries after the Aristotelian split had flawed the Greek concept of a unified whole, the Christian theologians battled for and achieved a doctrinal orthodoxy which was sufficiently powerful to defeat its rival religions and sects. It became the dominant religion of the Western world. Mohammedanism, the nearest neighbouring religion, derived much from Christianity but was not able to infiltrate Christian territories except by force. The church kept its converts, reinforced by the disciplined thinking of theologians who are still honoured today.

45. St Thomas Aquinas (detail, Traini) The star shedding light over St Thomas symbolises his enlightenment.

Virgin Penitents and Fallen Women

Celibacy is not purity. The early Christians equated their quest for purity with the state of celibacy, which was considered a prerequisite for eternal life. Women were relegated to an unimportant role also because people in those days believed that the end of the world was nigh and thus placed little value on womankind either biologically or socially. This view denigrated ordinary women as sex objects and deliberate temptresses; in reaction, virginity was venerated. The cult that developed around female virgin saints was a deliberate antidote to the weakness of the flesh.

The virginal cult was complicated by the traditional image of women as mother-figures. This paradox was exemplified by the Virgin Mary, venerated both for being innocent of sexual experience and as the mother of Jesus Christ. She is as close to being a demi-goddess as a monotheistic religion can permit and is revered as a being above the natural order, which places her above saints or angels, and is indeed a most exceptional cult in her own right. This was proclaimed by the papal bull of 1854, *Ineffabilis Deus*, in the form of the dogma of her Immaculate Conception which also exempted her from original sin and from temptation. It also reinforced the theory that she was second only to her divine son.

The incident of her annunciation in the scriptures has intrigued and titillated the Western world for nearly two thousand years. The humanisation of Jesus Christ by His birth to Mary created the dilemma for the Christian church of somehow having to rationalise convincingly the fact that the son of God was actually in her womb and consequently born to her, a mere woman. The virgin birth has disquieted ordinary Christians and theologians alike.

Of the other honoured virgins blessed with special powers St Audrey (Ethelreda), a princess of East Anglia, was the most venerated of Anglo-Saxon lady saints. Audrey's virginity was considerable – it survived two marriages. The first left her widowed and the second, to Egfried of Northumbria, ended when she persuaded her frustrated husband to annul the marriage. He agreed, but once Audrey left his court he pursued her hotly. The legend relates that she hid on a headland near Coldringham where the waters conveniently rose, surrounding her and blocking pursuit. There she stayed until her husband recognised that he had been thwarted by divine intervention. Later Audrey founded a double monastery at Ely, originally her dowry, where she was joined by some of the female members of her family. Even at court Audrey had been notably austere: cloistered, she enjoyed her

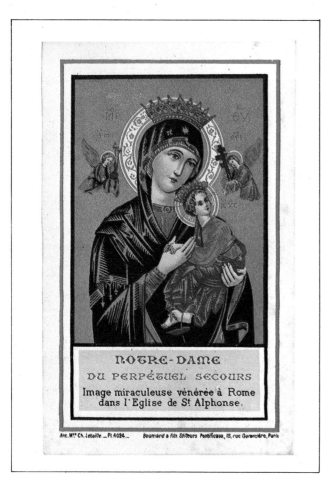

46, 47. Our Lady of Perpetual Succour *(left)* and **Our Lady of Luxemburg.** The Virgin Mary in two of her many roles as the powerful mother of Christ. These votive pictures are kept by the faithful as aids to prayers for her help.

penitential life of prayer, penance, rough clothes and only one meal a day. She died from a neck tumour which was thought to be divine punishment for wearing valuable necklaces during her youth at court; this was the origin of the word 'tawdry'. Her body was said to have remained uncorrupt and the tumour to have healed after her death.

The fifth century French virgin, St Genevieve, vowed perpetual chastity at the age of seven and took the veil when she was fifteen. Although bound to a pious and secluded life, Genevieve undertook a series of dramatic sorties from the cloister. Once when Paris was under siege by the Franks she led an armed band to gather corn for the starving Parisians, which act so impressed the enemy that they spared the prisoners. Another time Genevieve persuaded her fellow citizens not to desert their city but to pray and do penance in the face of the approaching army of Attila the Hun. Impressed by this unusual form of defence, Attila marched warily round Paris and went off to devastate a different area instead.

After her death Genevieve's body was enshrined in a church built by Clovis, the King of the Franks, who on conversion to Christianity announced that his subjects would also enjoy the new religion and ordered simultaneous baptism for all of them. Genevieve's relics were considered extremely powerful; once when Paris was stricken by the plague her feretory was processed round the city, which dispelled the sickness and all were saved. Genevieve is the patroness of Paris and her emblem is the candle.

Another saintly virgin, St Claire, was engaged to St Francis of Assisi but when she was eighteen she was jilted by the holy man in favour of My Lady Poverty. So she, too, renounced her worldly possessions and followed in her beloved's footsteps, eventually becoming the foundress of the Poor Clares. Her life of exemplary poverty and chastity was full of incidents which evidenced her special powers. Once when Assisi was threatened by the armies of the Emperor Frederick II, Claire was hurried from her sick-bed to the city walls to hold up the sacred host, before which his pagan mercenaries fled.

Claire's passion for mortification is said to have surprised even St Francis and her search for a life of perfect discomfort earned her the admiration of her fellow Assisians. Pope Innocent IV rushed to her death bed to administer the last rites to the esteemed virgin. Innocent was so enthusiastic about Claire's holiness that he had to be restrained from canonising her at her funeral. She was accredited with the power of bilocal sight – she could see places and events when she was actually elsewhere – and is thus, aptly, the patroness of television.

The first saint born in the New World to be canonised was St Rose of Lima. While very young Rose underwent an agonising operation which was said to have wakened her appetite for suffering. When people praised her beauty she would rub pepper on her face lest she should succumb to the sin of vanity. Refusing to consider marriage, Rose became a Dominican nun at the age of twenty and until her death in 1617 lived as a recluse in the family summer-house. There she performed her ritualistic penances of scourging, chewing bitter herbs, rubbing lime on her hands, not sleeping for days and fasting until anorexic. Visions and ecstasies followed penitential sessions. Rose wore a hair shirt and a silver circlet studded on the inside with thorns and dragged a heavy wooden cross around the garden. Eventually her family and friends became alarmed by her extravagant activities and an ecclesiastical enquiry revealed that Rose experienced regular visits from the devil.

Despite the evil visitations, her extraordinary psychological and physical contortions enhanced her image as a spiritual sufferer and firmly established

48. St Genevieve
(engraving after de Champagne) Owing to the powerful reputation of her relics, St Genevieve was invoked against public calamities.

56

49. *Above* **St Claire of Assisi,** holding the sacred monstrance which repelled the Saracen mercenaries during an invasion.

50. *Right* **St Rose of Lima,** who prayed for God to increase her sufferings so that she might do more glorious battle against the dangers of self-love.

Rose as the holy virgin of the New World. When she was not prostrate with exhaustion or in ecstasy, Rose cared for the poor and sick, an activity uncharacteristic of the ruling Spanish in Latin America. For this work she became venerated as the originator of social services in Peru. After her death several miracles were attributed to her intervention and her corpse was placed in a special chapel in the church

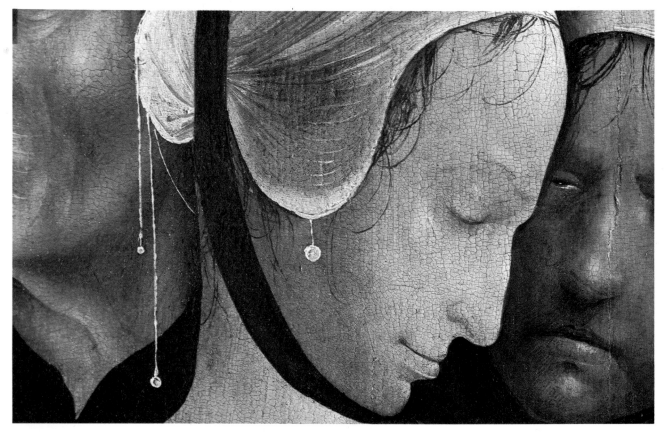

of St Domingo in Lima. Rose is the patroness of South America and the Philippines.

Her successor in the school of aggressive chastity was another South American virgin, St Marina de Jesus Paredes y Flores. Known as the Lily of Ecuador, Marina lived in Quito in the seventeenth century where as a child she punished herself with thorn bushes and prickly leaves. She chose to live as a recluse in a small room in her sister's house as a dedicated solitary virgin. Her only companion was the dummy of a corpse in a coffin which she kept as a reminder of death. Every Friday she would remove the dummy, get into the coffin

51. St Veronica (detail from The Carrying of the Cross, Hieronymous Bosch) Veronica wiped the sweat from the brow of Christ on the road to Calvary. An imprint of His face was left on the cloth, called Veronica's Veil.

herself and spend the night there, draping her arms and legs with chains and wearing an iron girdle around her waist which she complemented with a crown of thorns and iron spikes. She never slept for more than three hours and reduced her diet to one small piece of bread a day. During an earthquake, which was followed by an epidemic, Marina offered her life in expiation of mankind's sins but her offer was not immediately accepted. However she did die soon afterwards and was buried in a Franciscan habit which was put on over her Jesuit-style dress. Venerated as a holy virgin, Marina was not canonised until 1950.

For those women who had succumbed to sexual transgression redemption was still possible, for the Scriptures produced an archetype of the 'fallen woman' in Mary Magdalene, a prostitute, who was absolved, befriended and honoured by Jesus Christ. At their first meeting, when Jesus was dining at the house of a Pharisee, she entered the room and fell weeping at His feet; she kissed them and dried them with her long hair and anointed them with myrrh, whereupon Christ, telling the startled guests that they had just witnessed true repentance, forgave Mary her sins and bade her go in peace.

This incident is held to be a great example of God's mercy for the lowest of sinners. Mary had not actually harmed anybody but she was regarded as deeply sinful, which enhanced her repentance and also confirmed the inferiority of all women who fall prey to sexual sin. Mary was to enjoy a special friendship with Christ; she witnessed His Crucifixion and was the first person to be addressed by Him after the resurrection. The peculiar circumstances of her life gave rise to numerous apochryphal stories including one which involved her in an affair with Christ which spread widely during the early years of Christianity. Her cult became extensive and influential and by the middle ages she was firmly established as the most important female saint after the Virgin Mary.

Like the denials of St Peter and Christ's forgiveness of his cowardice, so the story of Mary Magdalene created a loophole which allowed a sinner to turn saint. The female penitents were noted

52. The Penitent Magdalene (woodcarving) Her penitence was to live a life of exemplary solitude. She was reputed to have survived to a great age on a mountain in Provence.

60

for their sins of impurity and vanity. They were reformed prostitutes, which role emphasised the belief that a woman who is neither virginal nor married must inevitably be to some extent immoral. Mary Magdalene was the warning and the hope, an example to Christian women that if they transgressed their proscribed roles they could be saved – but only by following her saintly example.

There were other splendid whores who repented conventionally and achieved sainthood. St Pelagia the Penitent was one, an erotic belly-dancer of Antioch who was famous for wearing fine pearls (earning her the nickname of Margarita). The lady's beauty obsessed a certain bishop, Nonnus, who commented that the attention Pelagia paid her looks was distinctly greater than that paid by the bishops to the souls of their flocks. Nonnus' appreciative eloquence converted Pelagia who was baptised and retired to a cave on the Mount of Olives, where she dressed in man's clothing and led a life of eremitical excellence.

A warm-hearted harlot who joined the saintly pantheon was St Mary of Egypt, a prostitute of Alexandria who had enjoyed a successful career from the age of twelve. At seventeen, Mary decided to make a pilgrimage to the Holy Land. Ever practical, she made herself available to the ship's crew and travelled as a working passenger. On arrival she visited the holy sepulchre where she kissed a piece of the true cross and was converted. Deciding to become a penitential hermit, Mary retired to the desert where she lived for fifty years. Even in solitude life held excitement for Mary, who was seen to levitate and to walk on water. During the middle ages she was a popular saintly penitent, sometimes

53. The Assumption of the Magdalene (Giulio Romano) Mary Magdalene was accredited with an assumption, a very high honour and sign of divine favour.

confused with Mary Magdalene as both were depicted as scrawny old hags with long, matted hair.

An equally intriguing conversion which must have raised the hopes of despairing women was that of St Thais. Thais was not only incredibly beautiful, she was also immensely rich. A holy desert monk called St Paphnutius decided to convert her which he achieved by 'having relations with her' at their first meeting which, remarkably, showed Thais the error of her ways. After making a public bonfire of her harlot's finery she entered a convent. She had not left her cell for three years when she was finally allowed to receive communion as a reward. Two weeks later Thais died.

In the legends and lives of the saintly virgins and repentant whores, the virgins are rewarded for their seclusion with special powers and the whores are rewarded for their retirement by veneration as holy penitents. Both cults involve women who are upheld as models of excellence when not sexually active. The church was incapable of suffering a threat to established definition of morality, hence women were excluded from the priesthood, from the sanctuary during mass, from church during menstruation and were 'churched' or readmitted to the congregation after having a baby. Holiness for women was therefore narrowly circumscribed and they were creatures to be despised like the whore, or excluded like the veiled nun. Even godfearing wives and mothers were accused of preferring the corrupting influence of family loyalties to communal needs.

Christianity displays an uneasy fear in its inability to accept the possibility of balanced sexual, familial and communal relations. The cult of the virgin penitents and reformed whores underlines an inequality of sex in a religion which officially declares that all its faithful are equal in the eyes of God: celibacy was cultivated, purity was sought, but at the expense of egality and understanding.

54. St Philip Neri (Algardi)
The founder of the
Oratorians, 'Pippo Buono'
received numerous
visitations including one
when the Virgin Mary
cured him of stones.

Visionaries and Mystics

The achievement of a state of self-awareness can be exciting and absorbing, for contemplation as a function of religious practice has induced states of awareness in practitioners which have been acknowledged as mystical experiences. Particularly noteworthy were visions and visitations thought to be either evidence of special attention by God or of temptation by the devil.

Through the traditions and tales of the fiery prophetic visions of the Old Testament, the story of Christ's life and resurrection and the reports of the ecstasies of the desert monks, Christianity became a religion with apparent recourse to divine communication through particularly holy individuals. This lent additional weight to spiritual directives to the faithful.

In 1380 the great mystic, Catherine of Siena, died at the age of thirty-three after a remarkably active life. The youngest of twenty children of a Sienese dyer, Catherine spent her childhood wearing a hair shirt and an iron girdle, fasting and praying in a cell and scourging herself daily. She joined the Dominicans and continued her life of solitude, often in states of ecstasy. After some years she emerged to nurse the sick and gradually acquired a following and a reputation as an enlightened commentator on religious and political matters. By the age of twenty-eight, she had become popularly accepted as a key figure in the return of the papacy to Rome from Avignon. Her threats of hellfire and criticisms of the church, especially the papacy, were combined with frequent travels around Italy to harangue political and religious leaders.

Catherine's pronounced effect on her contemporaries was due in part to her dominating personality and, also, to her prestige as a mystic. Although she never learned to write, she dictated an incessant flow of commentaries and directives and published her renowned *Mystical Dialogue* and letters. As holy virgin, who through mystical experience was enabled to apprehend truths automatically and without recourse to logic, Catherine was seen as an inspired example of spirituality. Her influence was augmented by the prevailing climate of uncertainty in Europe; the Black Death had ravished a quarter of the total population, and the corruption of the church was notorious. The majority were dismally convinced that the end of the world was at hand. The faithful sought evidence of divine reassurance and seemingly found it in her intrusive and bullying directives as to how they should better lead their lives.

Catherine was declared a doctor of the church long after her death and was also revered as a recipient of the stigmata which, although painful, were not visible until she died after a stroke in Rome. Her body was enshrined at SM Sopra Minerva and her head was taken back to Siena where it is still kept in her house.

The continuing corruption of the papacy helped to bring about the great schism of the Reformation and with it the Protestant denial of the

saintly role, which denial was hotly repudiated by Rome. The authorities reworked the saintly legends to give them a more acceptable scientific flavour. The cult of the saints was ratified by increased veneration and demonstration of their roles as receivers of divine communications.

One night in 1544, St Philip Neri experienced an ecstatic vision in the catacomb of St Sebastian in Rome. Divine Love, in the form of a globe of fire, entered his body through his mouth and on reaching his heart dilated it. This dilation was confirmed by post-mortem and presented as evidence of his experience, but dilation is known to be caused by heart disease and is common in old age. Philip died when he was eighty and was revered as an authority on the matter of visions. He instructed aspirants to test the nature of an apparition: 'If one appears in the guise of the Good Lord, but may really be a devil in disguise – it is best to spit on it. If the apparition then runs away, it is in fact the devil playing tricks.' This useful piece of advice was from the man who became the founder of the Oratorians, and the Apostle of Rome.

The most emphatic and articulate mystic of the Counter-Reformation was the Spanish Carmelite, St Teresa of Avila. Teresa was a Castilian who decided to enter the Convent of the Incarnation at Avila at the age of twenty. Although she claimed to find the life dissatisfying she stayed there for the next twenty-five years. Then in 1552 she founded the first reformed Carmelite convent, also at Avila, with the help of her friend and fellow mystic, St John of the Cross. Their work was hampered by two things. Firstly, the Carmelite establishment reacted strongly against the winds of change. In 1577 the Prior-General imprisoned John in a dark cell and visited

55. St Catherine of Siena (Vanni) Catherine received her stigmata in Pisa, when the blood-red rays emanating from a crucifix pierced her body.

64

56. The Ecstasy of St Teresa (Bernini)

him only to refuse personally his appeals for mercy. Secondly, public discovery of Teresa's mysticism and visions aroused such a stir that her superiors ordered her to write about them in an autobiography. For this and for her other writings, Teresa became the first woman to be honoured as a doctor of the church.

The descriptions of her visions are sensual and moving. She wrote of 'tasting' the 'great love of God' and her account of a visitation by an angel is revealing. 'He had in his hand a long golden dart; at the end of the point methought there was a little fire. And I felt him thrust it several times through my heart in such a way that it passed through my very bowels. And when he drew it out, methought it pulled them out with it and left me wholly on fire with a great love of God.' Teresa identified herself with St Mary Magdalene and St Augustine of Hippo – two saints who were venerated for their remorse for sexual sins. Her description of being carried off to hell is like a return to the womb through areas which are surely out of bounds to the celibate aspirant.

Teresa's approach to the problems of religious life was practical and intelligent. Nearly every description of her (and there are many) includes the words 'common sense'. She was witty, attractive and efficient. As the archetypal Christian mystic, St Teresa of Avila reaffirmed the doctrine of the Church of Rome.

An Italian contemporary of Teresa's, St Catherine dei Ricci, was another mystical bride of Christ. When she was nineteen Catherine had a vision of the Crucifixion which disturbed her so greatly that she retired to bed for three weeks, only to be revived by another vision of the risen Christ accompanied by the Virgin Mary and St Mary Magdalene. For the following twelve years in her convent in Tuscany Catherine spent every Friday – absolutely regularly – in ecstasy. When her weekly visitations were made public she became a celebrity and, as her influence

57. St Catherine Ricci (wood engraving)

increased, she identified herself with her temporal hero – Savonarola.

Catherine was blessed with the stigmata, complete with a wound on her left side and a crown of thorns burdening her brow. The pain caused by these phenomena sensitized her to the torments of souls in purgatory and she would offer to suffer vicariously for them. Her body was covered in blisters, emitting a heat so great that her cell seemed to be on fire. Her flesh appeared as if roasted and her tongue like a red-hot iron. During times of ecstasy a supernatural fragrance was emitted from her body and when Christ placed a ring on her finger there was a 'sweet singing of a multitude of angels'. Catherine's fellow nuns shared the pleasure of the heavenly perfumes which suffused the nunnery whenever she was in ecstasy. Catherine died in an odour of sanctity and was canonised a century and a half later, in 1747.

One of the most humourless saints ever canonised was a French nun, St Margaret Mary Alacoque (Voltaire was said to have delighted in her name). Between 1673 and 1675 Christ appeared to

Voilà ce Cœur qui a tant aimé les hommes!

58. St Margaret Mary Alacoque receiving the visitation of the Sacred Heart.

Margaret Mary four times, displaying His heart to her. Once it was burning like a furnace . . . at other times it was torn and bleeding 'on account of the coldness and the sins of men'. He would pluck it from His chest and hold it out to her. Why Margaret Mary should have been so honoured was a mystery to her fellow nuns. They found her a disconcerting companion, particularly when she announced that God had asked her to suffer for their sins. She was said to have been able to 'smell' sin in others, but the holy nuns thought that she was suffering from delusions of grandeur. Margaret Mary patiently bore with their scepticism and by the time she died they were converted to the idea of Christ transmitting special messages to their community. Their sympathetic conversion was promoted by her director and confidant, the Jesuit Jean-Claude la Colombière, who insisted that Margaret Mary's descriptions of her visions were read aloud to the nuns during their meals. Eventually her message was inaugurated as the devotional cult of the Sacred Heart. A highly influential and international organisation was founded in the nineteenth century using the emblem of a pink, cushion-like heart with flames coming out of the top which is still to be found in abundance in Catholic countries.

The most notable wonderworker of the eighteenth century saints was the ecstatic St Gerard Majella, a Redemptorist lay brother. Gerard started out as a tailor's apprentice, became a manservant to the bellicose Bishop of Lacedogna and joined the Redemptorists. For the last six years of his short but eventful life he acquired a reputation for exercising a remarkable variety of special powers. He could 'read' people's souls. There were more than twenty incidents when he made sinners repent by revealing their own wickedness to him. He had special communicative powers with inanimate objects and with the lower orders of animal life. He was given to ecstatic flight – one of his flights being reckoned at over half a mile. Gerard also had the gift of bilocation, but more than this, on one occasion while in retreat Gerard was visited by his rector who later

OFFRANDE AU SACRÉ-CŒUR

Je vous offre les misères de mon pauvre cœur. Renouvelez-le par le sang vivifiant qui coula du vôtre afin qu'il soit digne de votre amour.

760
E.BOUASSE JEUNE PLACE S.T SULPICE, 12, PARIS.

CHAPELET DU SACRÉ-CŒUR

GROS GRAINS: Doux Cœur de Jésus, soyez mon amour. 300 j. d'in. Doux Cœur de Marie, soyez mon salut. 300 j. d'indul.

PETITS GRAINS: Jésus, doux et humble de cœur, rendez mon cœur semblable au vôtre. 300 jours d'indulgence.

BOUASSE JEUNE   3657   PLACE S.T SULPICE, 19, PARIS.

Mon cœur fuira les Vanités pour se rapprocher de vous O Seigneur!

F. WENTZEL   278   PARIS

CŒUR SACRÉ DE JÉSUS

BOUASSE-LEBEL   PARIS

AYEZ PITIÉ DE MOI. (100 J.)

Vendredi

Consacrer son cœur à Jésus... c'est le consacrer au bonheur! Jésus mesure ses dons et ses faveurs, à l'étendue de notre Confiance.

R. Mère Barat.

Pratique

Consécration au Sacré Cœur de Jésus.

E. BOUASSE J.ne ÉD.   477 RUE MABILLON, 9.

60. St Gerald Majella

61. The Immaculate Medal 'O Mary, conceived without sin, pray for us who have need of you.'

complained to him that he had looked in his room but had been unable to find him. Gerard explained that he had asked God to make him invisible as he did not want to have his prayers interrupted. He died of consumption at midnight on 15 October 1755 – the exact hour he had predicted.

In 1831 a young Frenchwoman, Catherine Labouré, entered the novitiate of the Daughters of Charity at the Rue de Bac in Paris. During her time as a novice she experienced a series of visitations during which she received instructions from the Virgin Mary. The first apparition was of the heart of St Vincent de Paul. On three consecutive days it hovered above his feretory. On the first day it was white, on the second it was fiery, and on the third it was red and black and accompanied by a voice which spoke ominously of calamities about to overwhelm France. Then the Virgin Mary herself began to visit her. On one occasion she sat on the director's chair in the sanctuary of the chapel, which chair is still on display to pilgrims. On another, and more significant occasion, she appeared arrayed in celestial robes, standing on a globe and holding another in her hand. While poised in this position the Virgin Mary instructed Catherine to have a medal struck with the symbol of her heart together with that of her Son. Catherine followed her instructions and the Miraculous Medal is worn by many Catholics who firmly believe in its thaumatergic powers. Catherine was canonised in 1947 as the holy vehicle of the cult of the Miraculous Medal.

Nearly thirty years after Catherine's experiences, the Virgin Mary made another series of visitations at Lourdes in the Pyrenees. In 1858, Bernadette Soubirois saw a beautiful lady eighteen times who identified herself as the Immaculate Conception, and on her instructions Bernadette drank from a spring at her feet. Since that moment the spring has produced impressive amounts of what has come to be known as Lourdes water.

Bernadette was also instructed to build a church. The result was the basilica of Lourdes – the boom town of Catholic cures. Bernadette's simplicity and clear conviction impressed her contemporaries. She was an uneducated asthmatic with a limited imagination. Her description of the beautiful lady recalled the religious images in pastel shades which are still prevalent in Catholic churches and institutions. Her behaviour throughout the establishment of the shrine was, by all accounts, impeccable. Bernadette died when she was thirty-six after a painful and protracted illness and was canonised in 1933. The church stated that she was canonised for her simple piety and faith.

These mystics show the change from Catherine of Siena's harsh forbidding voice, the product of a climate of fear, to little Bernadette Soubirois' visitations by a beautiful, friendly lady. The faithful were given guidance by one of their own kind.

As to the value of the visions, perhaps this can be explained by the analogy of Mary Tudor's false pregnancy. Since she experienced all the expected symptoms it could be said that her pregnancy was real but not actual. Teresa of Avila's visions were real enough for her to describe them with an admirable conviction. Whether or not they actually happened is impossible to prove.

Mysticism is a perplexing question which Thomas Aquinas spent a considerable amount of time trying to define. Finally he declared that it is an attainment of truths through metaphysical reflection beyond reason. This notion – grand as it is – is a far cry from Bertrand Russell's that mysticism is, in essence, little more than a certain intensity of feeling in regard to what is believed about the universe.

The great Christian mystics were capable of intense feelings about their beliefs. Their faith was energetic and inspiring. Small wonder, then, that they impressed their contemporaries sufficiently to be accepted as the holy recipients of divine messages and understanding, and that they were and still are revered as supreme examples of the faithful.

62. Our Lady of Lourdes (plastic souvenir from the shrine)

**63. The Virgin and Child
with Sts Anthony Abbot
and George** (Pisanello)
The Hospitallers of St
Anthony were granted
special privileges, which
included carrying bells
and keeping pigs, which
were allowed to roam the
streets.

Monastics

Contemplation was an alternative religious life and expression of faith for those Christians who were not active proselytisers or martyrs. The materialism of the Roman empire followed later by the imperial promotion of Christianity as its official religion was not to the taste of those in search of ascetic and mystical fulfilment. Reverence of Christ as the 'Ultimate Sufferer' attracted them to a penitential existence, of living martyrdom in imitation of Him.

The caves of the Egyptian deserts were the homes of the original monks. They were influenced by the Judaic tradition of holy men living in the wilderness awaiting the Messianic arrival. The Diaspora of the Jews scattered the Christians too, who also refused to offer obeisance to Roman gods and, logically enough, were loath to pay taxes to them. Persecution increased the numbers of Christians who were drawn to places of silence, safety and solitude where through prayer, penance and poverty they attempted to attain a heightened state of spirituality in which they might achieve a closer union with God.

The acclaimed father of Christian monasticism was St Anthony the Anchorite of Egypt. At twenty he disposed of his worldly possessions and joined the local ascetics in the region of the Lower Nile. After some years as their disciple he moved further into the desert and complete solitude where, alone and unwashed, Anthony experienced a series of temptations. His personal struggle and eventual triumph was an epic moral tale of heroic asceticism versus the weakness of the flesh. In this battle with his unworthy physicality, Anthony forced himself to experience states of hyper-awareness conducive to mystical, revelatory consciousness which he promoted by starvation, lack of sleep, continuous silence and self-flagellation. Privation and humiliation were considered essential to the required subjugation. After years of struggling to be saintly, Anthony moved to a cave on Mount Kolzin, near the Red Sea. Groups of followers made their way to him to learn by example. By the time of his death, at the reputed age of 105, Anthony was famous both for his wisdom and exemplary penitence. On his instructions he was buried in a secret place, but such precious relics could not be left unexcavated and by the sixth century his bones were 'discovered' and shrines proliferated.

As the classic desert father St Anthony was less extreme in his lifestyle than many other early monks. In previous times the Jewish monks of Qumran were not allowed to defecate on the Sabbath as this was regarded as a form of labour (necessitated by the digging of a hole), which was forbidden. Christian monks attempted to dispel erotic thoughts by spending long nights in old, cold wells and, indeed, no form of filth, pain or discomfort was too great in their quest to subdue the flesh. But even this atrocious rigour did not avail, and aged monks continued to confess their physical and sexual preoccupations on their deathbeds. Unsuccessful attempts to repress sexuality started a fashion for

self-castration which became so widespread that the church had to forbid it. Early monks and hermits lived in penitential extremes only rivalled by those of the early martyrs.

St Anthony was venerated as the founder of eremitic, or Antonine, monasticism but another Egyptian, St Pachomius, was responsible for the founding of the alternative and eventually the more successful form – communal monasticism, known as cenobism. Pachomius was a contemporary of Anthony who also sought the purifying rewards of the solitary life and attracted a large following. He organised similarly sociable individuals into groups and catered for the needs of a greater variety of personalities. This made monasticism more readily available to aspiring Christians. His first monastery was founded in 320 and by the time of his death, twenty-six years later, he had founded seven monasteries for men and two for women.

During these years, St Pachomius compiled a book of Rules, later translated into Latin by St Jerome, which became the foundation of monastic Rule; both St Basil in the East and St Benedict in the West based their own monastic Rules on his book. Pachomius removed monasticism from desert solitude and introduced it into rural communities in which monks and nuns followed the contemplative codes and worked to be self-supporting as artisans. This new and more balanced approach could be sustained over longer periods than the life of the eremites and these cenobite monastics became the working class of the Christian church, although their system was considered heretical by the church hierarchy.

64. The Temptation of St Anthony (Ernst) Anthony was visited by hideous demons, offered creature comforts and tempted by luscious sirens.

While monks were organising the monastic system, enthusiastic individuals continued to lead eremitic lives. One of the most exotic of these was St Simeon Stylites, a solitary of great originality who retired to live on a pillar in 423, after a sojourn in the desert. At first he built a pillar of moderate height but he extended it repeatedly until he towered over his admiring disciples by some sixty feet. At the top there was a platform about twelve feet square complete with a balustrade from which he harangued his followers. A contemporary said of Simeon that 'despairing of escaping the world horizontally, he tried to escape it vertically'.

There were many varieties of dramatic eremitism. In the quest for sainthood, frantic solitaries starved themselves, induced agonising constipation, ate rotten food, leapt into beds of nettles or thorns, buried themselves and retired into murky pools or icy waters for months at a time. Pain was still equated with spiritual gain in their efforts to achieve an unearthly excellence.

While the hermits tried to solve the crisis of being mortal with immortal aspirations, a strange trio collaborated to further the monastic system. It comprised a rich Roman matron, St Paula, her daughter, St Eustochium and their avuncular spiritual superintendant, St Jerome. The teaming of Jerome's distinguished scholasticism, violent temper and preoccupation with chastity and St Paula's good works and piety riveted their Roman contemporaries. The women's association with Rome's self-appointed expert on chastity caused so much gossip that they emigrated to the Holy Land. There Paula founded a convent and financed the founding of a monastery. When she died Eustochium continued

to supervise the convent despite considerable debts left by her pious mother. But she too died soon afterwards and Jerome mourned them both. Through the efforts and wealth of the two women he had been able to apply his monastic theories which were highly influential in expounding the validity and and practicality of the scriptures as guidelines to the contemplative life. He placed especial emphasis on the perpetual virginity of the Virgin Mary as an essential example of spirituality.

Another great scholar who influenced monastic thinking was St Jerome's contemporary, St Augustine who, on becoming Bishop of Hippo in North Africa, organised a community which combined the contemplative life with the secular activities of the episcopal church. He assessed the problems and ideals of both forms of the religious life and introduced a Rule which is still employed by the Augustinian friars, the Canons Regular and by other male and female orders. Augustine was a skilled administrator and presided as religious leader over a community which was threatened with the collapse of its civil and cultural authority by the barbarian invasions. He, too, was obsessed with the concept of the innate sinfulness of man and so he re-emphasised guilt in the contemplative consciousness.

The struggle of the saintly contemplatives to find some method of coping with their overwhelming horror of human weakness, and at the same time to organise large groups of aspirants to spend their lives in an ordered version of the same pursuit, was eased by the innovation of a Rule by an Umbrian monk, St Benedict. This was chiefly a simplification of past Rules, and one which was long overdue: it discouraged the extremes of Eastern monasticism and forbade eremitism. The value of a sedentary stability was stressed in the initiation vows, which lessened roadrunning and mendicancy. Austerity remained the watchword and washing was not

65. St Paul of Thebes (Rosa) St Paul is venerated as the first Christian hermit, and lived for well over a hundred years.

encouraged, but Benedict's Rule emphasised the obvious need of most people to live life practically. In the light of current beliefs his idea of the enclosed life was revolutionary and is still in use today as the basis of most Rules throughout the Christian world.

66. St Benedict gave his monks six days notice of his impending death, and ordered them to dig his grave.

St Benedict is regarded as the patriarch of Western monasticism. But very little is known of him. He studied in Rome until the age of twenty, when he retired to Subiaco south of Rome. After attempting to discipline his unruly monks who were said to have tried to poison him (a poisoning from which Benedict miraculously recovered) he founded twelve communities. The last of these was the now famous monastery of Monte Cassino which he founded around 530. He was probably never ordained as a priest, but within his lifetime his reputation spread all over the Christian world.

Within the next two hundred years, the monastic missionaries who evangelised Europe disseminated an organised system of education which continued traditions of classical culture that might otherwise have vanished with the disintegration of the Roman Empire. The monks were the scholars responsible for the development of studies which started the medieval university system. One of the most popular of these academic monks was an obscure Englishman, known as the Venerable Bede.

St Bede was honoured as the most learned man of his time. He wrote voluminously on the scriptures and also compiled the first English history, which still intrigues scholars. Years of exemplary monkish life enabled Bede to study without interruption and he hardly ever ventured outside the cloister which clearly suited him, as he recorded, 'I have devoted my energies to the study of the scriptures, observing monastic discipline and singing the daily service in church; studying, teaching and writing have always been my delight.' Bede is especially famous in England and is considered the perfect example of monastic diligence and scholasticism subservient to Christian dogma.

By the twelfth century, the monasteries were the most powerful organisation in Europe, counterbalanced by the episcopal hierarchy of the papacy: Rome was still the unquestioned spiritual centre. A

67. St Romuald (engraving after Bourdon) Famous for his austerity, Romuald re-introduced the eremitic idea which had been rejected by the Benedictine Rule.

dramatic embodiment of the energies and paradox of monastic participation in temporal politics was the life of the fiery preacher and confessed mystic, St Bernard of Clairvaux. A Burgundian, Bernard Sorrel was one of the most influential personalities in the Christian church at the height of its power. At the age of twenty-two he persuaded thirty-one companions, including some unwilling members of his family, to join him at the Cistercian monastery at Citeaux. There Bernard started to reform the Cistercians, transforming them into an order which spread throughout Europe, until there were nearly five hundred communities at the time of his death. They observed an austere monastic life, clinging to the old values of manual labour and prayer. On becoming Abbot of Citeaux, Bernard exhorted his companions to 'gird their loins and grasp the nettle' of hard work. But they objected to his prescribed diet of barley bread and boiled beech leaves and thus his desire for a return to an even more stringent monastic life was thwarted.

Although Bernard often declared that he would have liked to have spent his entire life in meditation he certainly did not spend much of it in a cell. He swept round Europe preaching moral reform and participating in power politics with Machiavellian dexterity. Bernard bullied the papacy, manoeuvred kings and bishops and was instrumental in the downfall of Peter Abelard, whose views contradicted his own. In merging the return to the old ideals with an obvious display of political power Bernard demonstrated the combination of worldliness and holiness which had become the dynamic of monastic endeavour. As contemplatives, monks were the accepted examples of spiritual excellence and simultaneously, as the most highly developed communal organisation, they had become systematically richer and thus more powerful. Bernard is honoured as an influential reformer of monasticism, though his writings have been described as 'pre-scholastic'.

Nevertheless, he is also esteemed as a doctor of the church and known as 'Doctor Mellifluous' or the 'Honey-sweet Teacher'; his emblem is a beehive.

Another reformer of medieval monasticism, St Bruno, also combined a solitary life with religious politics. His personal crusade was against the increasing corruption of the monks and clergy. In 1084, at Grand Chartreuse, he founded the Carthusian order whose aim was to return to the eremitical life in reaction to the increasing laxity of the Benedictine Rule. When he was summoned to Rome as an advisor to Pope Urban II, Bruno began to live in the ruins of Diocletian's baths as a hermit when not summoned to the papal elbow. He believed in the positive power of holiness as an antidote to his contemporaries' behaviour. He demanded that his Carthusians should lead a life of poverty which emphasised the same penitence that had preoccupied the ancient hermits of the Egyptian desert. His insistence on a strict interpretation of the monastic ideal continued to attract a considerable following and the Carthusians were soon firmly established as a strong influence within the church. Bruno was venerated as an upholder of the early principles of a life dedicated to the imitation of Christ.

The development of the saintly ideal, from St Anthony wrestling with the devil in the desert to the sophisticated manoeuvres of the medieval saints, spanned one thousand years and illustrates the evolution of the saintly search for spiritual excellence. The medieval monks declared their desire for a life of contemplation, but they lived in a society which compelled those who had acquired a reputation for holiness to display that holiness publicly. So, paradoxically, the leaders and innovators of the monastic search for a means of obtaining and keeping an ideal contemplative life were the very people most sought after by the outside world.

St Bernard and St Bruno understood their power as spiritual leaders, used it to the full and

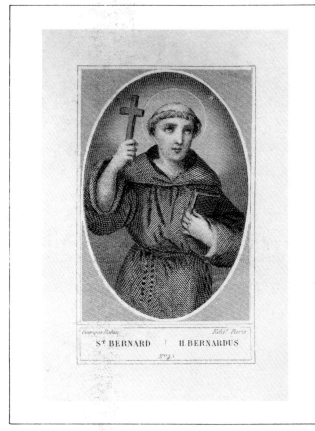

68. St Bernard (prayer card)

69. *Right* **St Bruno** (lithograph after Le Sueur) The saint is shown refusing Pope Urban XI's offer of an archbishopric.

in so doing demonstrated the increasing need for members of religious orders to work outside the cloister. The founding of the Dominican and Franciscan orders by Sts Dominic and Francis, contemporaries of St Bernard, began a movement towards the organisation of religious orders as workers in the outside world. Later, the great upheavals of the

Reformation and Counter-Reformation revitalised the missionary and educational zeal which included the introduction of more sociable secular activities as a practical part of the religious ideal. The monasteries thus became less important and less powerful, but they continued to exist as an established option in the Christian church and today they are to be found all over the world. With an increasing interest in oriental religions and methods of contemplation, Christian monasticism is now attempting a type of ecumenical face-lift in the hope of attracting more young converts.

The cult of the contemplative saints re-affirms the monastic way of life as a genuine search for holiness. The crucial problem, of a search for peace in which contemplation is frequently and deliberately interrupted by penitential struggles to subdue the demands of the flesh, has remained constant and has always created tensions and distractions. It is difficult to assess to what extent monks discovered an inner peace with God if they had to starve to do so. Notwithstanding, the monastic saints were glorified for this struggle to find a closer union with their maker.

70. St Bernard's Vision of the Blessed Virgin Mary (Filippino Lippi)
The 'honey-sweet' teacher in a painting by the son of an illegal union between a monk and a nun.

Founders

St Dominic and St Francis of Assisi founded monastic orders on the principle of mobility rather than seclusion, in response to the changing needs of the expanding and increasingly urban Christian communities of the middle ages.

At the beginning of the thirteenth century, a Spanish deacon called Dominic Guzman was a member of a papal mission sent to the south of France to deal with the Albigensians, an heretical sect which had hitherto successfully resisted interference from church officials. The irony of well-fed monks carrying the standard of the established church against a community of dedicated ascetics was not lost on Dominic. Taking as a model the early Christian missionaries, he established a company of peripatetic friars. Believing that 'a man who governs his passions is the master of the world. We must either rule them or be ruled by them. It is better to be the hammer than the anvil', Dominic trained his followers as preachers. Instead of leading a cloistered, agricultural existence they were sent out to be a more persuasive psychological alternative to the established methods of the physical suppression of heresy.

The Dominicans adapted the basic Augustinian Rule and joined the faculties of European educational institutions, which they soon dominated. The Dominican emphasis on learning and its intellectual approach to religious studies helped to

S. DOMINICUS.

71. St Dominic with a dog holding a burning torch in its mouth as a symbol of Dominic as the herald of truth.

revitalise Christian thinking. The Dominicans were energetic inquisitors – among them the Grand Inquisitor Torquemada – and soon their black and white habits came to symbolise the punishments in store for those suspected of heresy. Dominic's following spread throughout Europe during his lifetime and thereafter into Asia and the New World. He was canonised thirteen years after his death and has been venerated ever since as the father of the watchdogs of medieval Christianity.

In marked contrast, St Francis of Assisi, an Italian contemporary, founded an order which introduced a completely different type of religious life. Taken prisoner during a war between Perugia and his home town, Francis was converted from an attractive young blood into a charismatic leader. Returning home, he dismayed his family, friends and fiancée – St Claire – by renouncing his worldly possessions and former ways to wed 'the fairest of all brides, My Lady Poverty'. Stripping himself of his finery, he retired to a ruined chapel and lived the life of a beggar, yet retained his personality and style. He soon attracted an enthusiastic following, drawn by his preaching of the simple Christian message of brotherly love, and within three years Pope Innocent III approved the founding of the Franciscan Order of the Friars Minor.

Francis' predilection for a life of total poverty, humility and charity was too extreme for his fellow Franciscans and a more conventionally comfortable Rule was evolved. Despite these basic changes, the order attracted such a wide following that church authorities became alarmed and restricted the Franciscans to preaching against usury, luxury, sodomy, vanity and vengeance.

72. St Francis of Assisi (detail, Rubens) He is the newly-appointed patron of ecology.

Francis was an original; his simple, joyous embracing of a more natural interpretation of religion was a refreshing contrast to the prevailing ecclesiastical culture which was marked by complicated ceremony overladen with guilt. Francis' view of God as the benevolent creator, coupled with his love of His creatures, anticipated the spirit of Renaissance Humanism. His was an eccentric ability to grasp an idea and to act on it without regard for contemporary opinion. Typically, he visited the Christian armies of the fifth crusade in 1219 to preach the pacifist alternative. His efforts were rebuffed and so he turned to the Muslim camp who were also not much impressed although their leader, Sultan Malik-al-Kamal, received him with the courtesy due a holy man.

The popular view of St Francis is one of a naïf and animal-lover, but he must also have been a highly persuasive individual who brought re-assurance to the sick and the poor with whom he identified and for whom he cared unceasingly.

Three hundred years after St Francis' death a grim figure brought the peripatetic missionary effort full circle with a return to the sterner elements of the Dominican ideal. St Ignatius of Loyola was a conquistador, a Spanish aristocrat with a very real sense of his own importance, who became convinced of his special destiny as a soldier of Christ while recovering from an excruciating leg wound. His new beliefs drove him to a long period of contemplation, during which he conditioned himself mentally and physically for total commitment. Subsequently, at Manresa near Montserrat, Ignatius wrote the first draft of his *Spiritual Exercises* which became the basis of the Jesuit method of religious conditioning. A quasi-military regime, featuring obsessive self-abasement redolent of hell-fire, it was premised on the total orientation of the mind and body to the requisite degree of dedicated commitment.

After a pilgrimage to Jerusalem, Ignatius

returned to Spain to study Latin and theology. His personal austerity and his practice of counselling the troubled, particularly women, attracted official notice and he was imprisoned as a suspected heretic. Upon his release he moved to Paris to continue his studies and found that his religious activities appealed to a group of followers who took the vows of poverty, chastity and papal obedience. In 1540 the Jesuits were formed and declared themselves ready to propagate the faith as required. Ignatius became the first general of the Society whose bold motto was, 'For the greater glory of God.' This secretive, elitist and puritanical group became synonymous with Rome's response to pre-Reformation decadence and the post-Reformation struggle between Catholics and Protestants in Europe.

In total contrast another Spaniard, St John of God, founded the Brothers Hospitaliers in 1539, which company was to become famous for introducing a new, more sympathetic approach to nursing. Originally a mercenary and then a shepherd, John became a religious enthusiast at the age of forty. His first missionary effort was a frustrated attempt to succour Christian slaves in North Africa in the hope of personal martyrdom. Dissuaded by friends, John settled in Granada where he peddled sacred books and pictures. This quiet respite was interrupted when, inspired by a sermon of John of Avila, a famous and compelling preacher, he dashed into the streets tearing his hair, beating his breast and shouting for mercy. His demented behaviour terrified the locals who pelted him with stones. Undeterred, John gave away his stock of books and roamed the streets of Granada. After a brief and well-merited spell in an asylum he determined to care for the poor and the

74. **St John of God** receiving his habit from the Bishop of Tuy.

sick. He rented a house which he filled with ailing paupers whom he supported by selling wood. His choice of patients – harlots and varlets – distressed some but impressed others, including the Bishop of Granada who endowed him with a religious habit. John died following an illness caused by his rescue of a drowning man and a Rule was

73. **The Apotheosis of St Ignatius of Loyola** (detail, Pozzo)

approved for his followers who were ordered as the Brothers Hospitaliers. John of God is the patron of hospitals and the sick and is especially venerated by booksellers.

After the Thirty Years War, the church still functioned as the official religious institution with attendant emphasis on secular comfort for its hierarchy at the expense of its congregation. It was not until a handful of people attempted to redress the balance that any real notice was taken of obvious inequalities. St Vincent de Paul was the most remarkable of these. A fashionable cleric and a court chaplain, his emotional concern for the poor was perhaps promoted by his own experience of unjust accusation when a young man. He travelled widely through France talking and listening to the poor people of the land, whose despair touched him, and resorting to his court contacts, most notably the Regent, Anne of Austria, Vincent collected funds for redistribution among the poor.

As an urbane skilled confessor, he was able to relate both to the problems of the powerful and of the deprived. His ability to make this connection across the social scale enabled him to reintroduce the practice of charity, which he formalised in his foundation of the Lazarites and the Daughters of Charity. Vincent applied the biblical maxim, 'Thou art thy brother's keeper', which then became the cornerstone of church philanthropy. Vincent is one of France's most honoured saints and his congregations are still active worldwide.

The alternative activity to proselytising through charity was education, which was available only to a fortunate few. The Dominicans and Jesuits mainly taught rich boys – girls and poor children were not considered educable. However, the idea that

75. St Charles Borromeo (Consadori) As the stuttering Bishop of Milan, Charles applied the reforming principles of the Council of Trent to re-organising education and pastoral care within the diocese.

girls ought to grow up to become effective Christian consorts and mothers implied a need for suitable preparation.

The first order founded to educate females was established by an Italian orphan, Angela Merici. In 1535 she and a group of like-minded females congregated in the church of St Afra at Brescia to dedicate themselves to this cause in the manner of the virgin penitents, and became the first House of the Company of Ursula. Initially they did not wear habits, take vows or live together, but later the Ursulines became more regimented. Angela was an independent and serious educationalist with a practical attitude untypical of her sex in the Renaissance period. Although she is now honoured as the foundress of this first and most effective order of women teachers, St Angela paid the price for thinking and acting in advance of her time; she died in 1540 but was not canonised until 1807.

Her example was followed seventy-five years later when two friends of St Vincent de Paul founded the first House of the Visitation. Two lonely aristocrats, Jane de Chantal and Francis de Sales, had begun a platonic affair when Jane, newly widowed, was directed towards religion by Francis, a distinguished theologian. He had hoped to form a company of nuns comprising single or widowed women of delicate health who would lead a plain but comfortable life including work outside the cloister. However, the nervous conservatism of the local bishop prompted by Lutheran attacks on strange activities in nunneries forced the Order of the Visitation to remain closed. This became characteristic of the female orders and endured into the twentieth century. By the time Jane died, over eighty Convents of the Visitation had been set up. Although she and Francis had failed to establish the type of institution they envisaged, their success must have been some small consolation.

The continuing need for improvement in

76. St Vincent de Paul
who is the special patron
of all charitable
associations.

77. St Angela Merici (engraving by Baquoy)

78. St Jane de Chantal receiving the Rules of the Order of the Visitation from St Francis de Sales.

education was obvious to Jean Baptiste de la Salle, one of the most distinguished educationalists to enter the Catholic clergy. Destined for the church almost from birth, Jean was tonsured when he was eleven and became a canon of Rheims at sixteen. Ten years later he rejected the life accorded a church aristocrat and, after his ordination, devoted himself to the education of the poor. He exasperated his fellow teachers by expecting them to follow his example of sharing his privileges with his pupils. Jean was undismayed by his colleagues' rejection and started to train the first Brothers of the Christian Schools. In 1686 the first teacher-training college was established on fundamental educational principles which were not much improved on in the next two hundred years; tuition in Latin was

91

replaced with the vernacular, silence in the classroom was still absolute, but a milder, more parental, approach towards the students was encouraged. Today the Christian Brothers are a worldwide order of teachers, and their founder is remembered for his contribution to education.

A major innovation in Catholic education was brought about in the nineteenth century by Dom John Bosco from Piedmont. Expanding educational opportunity beyond the traditional classroom, he organised technical schools and extra-curricular activities to improve the lives of the poor boys of the overcrowded cities of northern Italy. His efforts made him a hero of the working classes and he was adulated by poor Italians who could not have been expected to see beyond the pietistic attitude of the contemporary church. His teaching accepted the idea that humility was a prerequisite for the humbly-born. He was a living legend and was canonised forty-six years after his death.

The founding saints have always been honoured by the church as instruments of the development of its social and educational activities which were formerly the province of monastics. They also established institutions which, although innovative at the time of their inception, became supportive of the traditional hierarchy. They re-activated the church's recruiting and indoctrinating, through education and nursing, in original and some-times radical ways. The power of Rome has been sustained by the institutions of its founding saints.

79. St John Bosco

Missionaries

The image of the missionary as the staple diet of central African cuisine is a by-product of the most successful evangelising campaign in history. St Paul transformed the Messiah from his role as hero of a Jewish sect to the saviour of mankind. Christianity became a multi-national religion whose potential congregation encompassed the entire population of the known world. The spreading of the Word was always an essential Christian duty.

The Diaspora of the Jews also dispersed the Christians from their first centre at Jerusalem, as they too refused to ally themselves with the official religion of the Roman Empire, declaring that their religion was not subject to temporal power. As they scattered throughout the Empire, the early Christians spread their message with eschatological haste. Making converts when and where they could, their following steadily increased. When, in the fourth century, Constantine declared Christianity the official religion of the Empire, Christian proselytising was thus sanctioned. With the gradual disintegration of the Empire and then the barbarian invasions, missionaries looked further afield than the Mediterranean. They began to push north and west from Rome and north and east from Byzantium to convert the scattered tribes, who had already rejected Roman rule.

The early missionaries ventured into regions inhabited by primitive peoples unused to the comparatively sophisticated structure of Mediterranean civilisations.

Christianity had to be translated back into simple beliefs unencumbered by theological organisation. Every missionary faced hardship and danger; many were killed. Gradually they met with more success and eventually the converted Christianised countries venerated their most effective apostles and adopted them as their national patron saints.

Gaul became a centre for these European missionaries. Among them St Martin of Tours, a Roman legionary stationed there, has been hailed as the father of French monasticism. The story of his conversion is familiar. One bleak winter's day Martin was leading his troops out of Amiens when he saw a beggar shivering with cold. Quickly cutting his cloak in two he presented the beggar with one half, wisely keeping the other for himself. Later in a dream the beggar was revealed to him as Jesus Christ who appeared wearing His half of Martin's cloak. Martin was baptised a Christian and applied for discharge from the army declaring that as a spiritual soldier of Christ he could no longer fight in the temporal legions of Rome. Soon he became a disciple of Hilary of Poitiers, a distinguished theologian famed as the 'Athanasius of the West' because of his eloquent defence of orthodoxy against the Arian heresy. Subsequently, Martin established the first French monastery at Ligurge, where he had settled as a solitary and had attracted a following. Twelve years later he was appointed Bishop of Tours but continued to live in a cell as an ordinary monk. He also

80. St Martin of Tours
(limewood statue)

founded the large monastery of Marmontier.

As a holy man in the public eye, Martin lived out his faith, always dressing as a monk as an example to his fellow bishops of the Christian principle of equality. The bishops had already gained privileges as the queen bees of the clergy, while the monks were only the workers. Martin established a string of monasteries in the countryside, where Christianity had not yet taken root, from which zealous monks set forth to propagate the faith. Despite a reputation for destroying trees and natural shrines sacred to the local gods he was strongly opposed to the death penalty for the practice of pagan rites, and found in the grafting of existing heathen practices onto the new religion a solution to the problem of satisfying the local patterns of ceremony and belief. He was indisputably a remarkable personality whose achievements have been exaggerated by enthusiastic biographers who have turned him into a holy giant dispensing miracle-cures with saintly ease. He became one of the most popular saints of medieval Europe and, in France alone, there are four thousand parish churches and five hundred villages dedicated to him. His shrine at Tours was a centre of Frankish pilgrimage.

While Martin was presiding over southern Gaul, a young Briton called Patrick was carried off to Ireland by pirates where he worked as a swineherd. After years of slavery he escaped and returned to his homeland via Gaul. Then Patrick had a dream in which he was told to return to Ireland to spread the gospel. Over the next fourteen years Patrick studied and prepared for his mission to Ireland, and finally landed there as a bishop in 432. Although he was not the first missionary to go to Ireland, it was Patrick who organised a national church along episcopal lines in a country which was not yet united. He was a tough and energetic proselytiser with the strength to confront the local chiefs and druids throughout thirty years of constant travel and

81. St Patrick (contemporary plastic statue)

95

incessant preaching in a country which has always delighted in speech-making.

The legends which arose from his deeds transformed him into a Titan who herded an entire nation into his pastoral flock, performing enough miracles to satisfy even the Irish. Of these, his most helpful and best-known was the expulsion of all snakes from the island. He is the patron saint of Ireland and is usually depicted wearing green vestments, a mitre, stamping on snakes or brandishing his crosier at them.

One hundred years after Patrick's death, thirteen Irish monks set sail for the island of Iona off the west coast of Scotland, under the leadership of Columba. A formidable evangeliser and an eloquent bard, Columba had the dubious reputation of having incited the bloody monastic battle of Cooldrew by appropriating a valuable psalter which he flatly refused to return. On Iona, a bleak place with a primordial atmosphere, Columba founded a monastery which became the focus for missionary efforts in Scotland and the north of England. Undeterred by the ferocious Picts of Scotland, who had terrified even the most seasoned of the Roman legionaries, Columba and his monks infiltrated the north and established and ruled the nascent Celtic church. Columba became a legendary figure in local history by banishing a terrible sea-monster from the river Ness to humour the powerful King Brude, who promptly converted. The Irish monks were especially noted for their stern and penitential practices and Columba himself was reputed to have fasted all the year round. Columba founded the Irish monastic missionary tradition in a country of savage, quarrelsome warriors, which tradition was carried to the Continent by his followers, but Iona remained one of the most famous monastic and spiritual centres in Europe.

St Columban was the most controversial of his followers; an archetypal Irish monk who in-sisted on penitence and was an intransigent proponent of the Irish approach to religious life. While Continental missions were led by monks who followed the more moderate Roman monastic tradition, formalised by the Rule of St Benedict, the Irish had adopted the extremist religious approach of the Eastern monks and had added their bardic practice of haranguing the congregations, cursing and swearing, and urging repentance with vehement threats of hellfire and damnation.

It is said that Columban became a monk after experiencing torrid carnal temptation, an experience he never forgave himself. A scholarly Leinsterman, Columban studied until he was nearly fifty under St Comgall, the founder of Bangor Abbey, who was well-known for his austere habits. He then left Ireland for Europe with twelve followers and established three monasteries in the Vosges, where he attracted a large following. This early success was short-lived, for Columban provoked the criticism of the church, and even that of Pope Gregory himself, by his insistence on the Irish Rule and angered the state with his refusal to bless bastards of the Frankish royal family. With church and state thus united in opposition, Columban and his Irish monks were deported. When a storm blew them back to the Continent, the rowed up the Rhine to Bregenz on Lake Constance where they were as unwelcome as in France. They crossed the alps and settled at Bobbio in Lombardy. As the local ruling family was at odds with the papacy, Columban's flagrant advance into Italian territory was tolerated, though he soon insinuated himself into local ecclesiastical arguments, which were the breath of life to him.

Columban is remembered as an inspired and well-educated missionary, but his cult has had to

82. Sts Patrick, George, Andrew and David (engraving with aquatint, after Egerton, 1827) The patron saints of the British Isles.

bear the legacy of his literal application of the Irish Rule which, although appealing to some, was generally considered extreme and gradually lapsed in favour of the Benedictine Rule. Columban's abrasive hellfire campaign through Europe proved counter-productive to his mission as, in reaction, a moderate system developed which became the backbone of a united Christendom.

Rome was not idle while the Irish evangelised. St Gregory the Great saw transalpine Europe as ripe for conversion. His most successful missionary venture was that led to Britain by Augustine, later known as St Augustine of Canterbury, the apostle of the English. Augustine was sent off by him to England, with a company of thirty monks and not much confidence. Gregory had to make him a bishop on his journey across Gaul to encourage them to continue. They managed to land in Kent where Augustine was granted an audience with the local king, Ethelbert, whose wife was a Christian. The

" Non Angli sed Angeli forent si fuissent Christiani.'

83. *Left* **St Gregory** (Leech) On seeing the English slaves in the market in Rome, he declared that they would be angels not Angles if they were Christian.

84. *Above* **St Augustine** before King Ethelbert, who agreed to confront the saint at an open-air gathering to discredit Augustine's reputed magical powers.

meeting was a great success; Augustine was granted land at Canterbury where he built a monastery and maintained it as his see when he was consecrated Archbishop of the English. Thus Canterbury became the seat of the primates of the English church. Augustine survived for only eight years, but in this time he established the seat and structure of the British church. In 664, at the Synod of Whitby, the English and northern Celtic churches settled their differences and became a united Christian church. It was at that Witenagemot, the deliberative assembly of the time, that such burning questions as the date of Easter and the manner of tonsure were sorted out.

Augustine's successful evangelising campaign was largely due to Gregory's interest and encouragement. Although Rome was a great distance from Canterbury (a distance that was to increase) Gregory advised him continuously and Augustine carried out his instructions with care, creating a Christian centre that was directly connected to Rome, but independent of its Gallic neighbours. Both Gregory and Augustine were revered as the special patrons of the English church.

At the beginning of the eighth century an English monk, Boniface, left England for Frisia, where he hoped to evangelise the ferocious natives. This proved a difficult task, so Boniface turned his attention to the tribes of Germany where he set about persuading the heathens there that his God was more powerful than their local gods. As proof, Boniface swept into the sacred shrine of Thor in Hesse and felled the Great Sacred Oak with one mighty blow of his axe, helped by a convenient gust of wind. This awesome act promoted a rash of conversions, after which Boniface left for Thuringia, armed with a battery of holy relics supplied from Rome, which he substituted for the abandoned magical charms of the new converts. Not only did Boniface convert a succession of German tribes,

he also founded and staffed a chain of monasteries which became the local centres for Christian learning.

In less than twenty years, Boniface consolidated a large section of the Christian church on the Continent, organised a church complete with a monastic and episcopal system, and integrated it with the Frankish and Italian churches. He achieved this by requesting and receiving continuous support from the church in England who supplied him with monks and money, by visiting Rome to report on his missions and to secure his position among his fellow churchmen, and by assisting the Frankish kings in their reformation of the church in France. When he was nearly eighty, Boniface gave up active direction of the German and the reformed French churches and returned to Frisia, still keen to convert the unwilling Frieslanders. Tragically, on the banks of the river Borne, they attacked him while he was reading in his tent and stabbed him to death.

Admired by his contemporaries as a teacher and acclaimed their most effective leader, Boniface became the most powerful churchman in Europe, after the Pope. As an entrepreneur of Christianity, the associate of popes and the advisor of kings, he welded together a church which transcended borders and feuds of ill-defined and unsettled territories, of warrior kings and troublesome tribes. His unifying mission helped to create a Christian Europe in the north, which was realised politically when Charlemagne was crowned and anointed Holy Roman Emperor.

By the ninth century, both the Roman and Byzantine churches had spread over much of the known world. Although they expanded in different directions, clashes were unavoidable. One instance of collision was when two brother missionaries, Sts Cyril and Methodius, evangelised Moravia in the Byzantine tradition, to the indignation of the German bishops. They imprisoned Methodius for two years, charging him with heterodoxy. The brothers became

+ B. Petrus Sanz socios suos B.B. Franciscum Serrano, Joachim Royo, Joannem Alcober et Franciscum Diaz ad martyrium adhortatur.

85. *Above* **Blessed Peter Sanz** and his fellow martyrs, a group of Dominican missionaries who were martyred in China during the eighteenth century.

86. *Right* **St Vincent Ferrar** (Cossa) A 'revivalistic' missionary in southern Europe in the fourteenth century, Vincent's hellfire sermons inspired a zealous following.

100

venerated by both the Eastern and Western churches as the apostles of the Slavs and were credited with the invention of the Glagolitic (later the Cyrillic) alphabet, with which they translated the liturgy and some of the scriptures into the vernacular. Belatedly, Methodius was made a patron of ecumenism.

With Europe successfully evangelised, the cult of missionary saints waned until the discovery of the New World presented new opportunities for heroic ventures. The Reformation and the spread of colonialism started a sectarian, nationalistic race for conversions. While the Protestants were occupied with internal dissensions and the redefining of their religious codes, the Roman Church was first in the field.

Among the new wave of missionaries was the Basque, St Francis Xavier, who embarked on a missionary journey which has tantalised Rome with the prospect of evangelising the Orient ever since. While a student in Paris, Francis became a friend and follower of St Ignatius Loyola. As a founder member of the Jesuits he dedicated himself to the missionary ideal, and in 1541 the King of Portugal commissioned him to go to the East Indies. He set sail for the Portuguese colony of Goa, in India, which became his headquarters. Dismayed by the corruption of Portuguese rule and the pitiful conditions of the natives, which made 'a permanent bruise on his soul', Francis only permitted himself the meanest existence, identifying himself with the oppressed lower castes.

Although Francis was prone to seasickness and had no facility for languages, for the ten years of his missionary journey he travelled incessantly through India and to Malacca and Japan, preaching a simplified version of the Christian doctrine. His keenness to approach the intricacies of the diverse cultures which he encountered increased the numbers of his converts almost to the miraculous.

This was complemented by an engaging personality and a genuine concern for suffering. Francis was instinctively recognisable as a holy man in the Eastern tradition and was thus enabled to perform mass baptisms of converts who responded to him even though the details of his evangelistic message were not necessarily fully understood.

After his time in India and Malacca, Francis spent two years in Japan where he was well, if cautiously, received. By the time he left, there were nearly two thousand Japanese Christians. Later they were severely persecuted; many were martyred and Christianity was driven underground. Finally Francis died at the age of forty-six on the island of Shangchwan, off the coast of China, which country had always been his ultimate goal.

At the court of Versailles during the seventeenth century preferred reading matter included the records of the Jesuit mission in Canada. This mission, led by Paul Lejeune, proposed to convert the Huron Indians who tolerated the missionary presence but were content with their own gods. The Jesuits persisted and lived among them in conditions of isolation, hunger and depressing squalor, until eventually their preaching began to take effect.

The Iroquois, traditional enemies of the Huron, regarded the missionaries in their sinister, long, black soutanes as targets for unusually vicious attacks. Some of the missionaries had their fingers gnawed by their captors and their nails torn out, while others were mutilated, dismembered and eaten. One priest, Anthony Daniel, a painter of scenes of missionary and Indian life, was flayed and his blood was drained and drunk. Jean de Bréboeuf, the Ajax of the group, had a necklace of red-hot tomahawks strung around his neck, following which he was 'baptised' in boiling water and, as he died, his blood was drunk by his captors who hoped to assume his courage. His heart was

87. *Above* **St Francis Xavier** (wood engraving after Deghouy) He was accredited with the gift of tongues, which allowed people of all nationalities to understand him when he preached.

88. *Right* **St Francis Xavier** lying in the church of Bom Jesu in Goa, where pilgrims still flock to kiss his miraculously preserved body. His right arm was removed and taken to Rome, and it has also been shown in America.

MICHAEL NACAXIMA *Iaponois, vande Societeyt IESV, opden 25 December Anno 1628. ende andere verscheyden soo Religieuse, als wereltsche persoonen, tot 31 toe, op verscheyden waeren, van hooghe rotsen ghewoorpen voor t'gheloof, in siedende, en solpherachtige wateren.*

eaten by the chief. This group of missionaries is venerated as the North American martyrs. In spite of such examples of native rejection of interference from the conquering Europeans, a century later the French exalted the notion of the noble savage.

After the evangelisation of the Americas and scattered areas of India and Asia, the African interior and the Pacific basin remained the largest potential areas for proselytisation. The political decline of the Catholic countries of Europe and the colonial ascendancy of Protestant nations changed the focus of missionary activities. The nineteenth century saw a missionary boom which was part of a period of intensive Western expansion. Evangelistic expeditions were strongly nationalistic and were inevitably involved with the race for the colonies. These missions were led by fervent evangelists who were sometimes party to the more dubious aspects of economic, and even military, domination. Their religious status permitted them a particular licence, nevertheless there was a considerable number who dedicated themselves with genuine altruism to the spreading of the gospel to the natives of those countries opened up by Western domination.

An example of this type of missionary to be venerated was the martyr of the New Hebrides, St Peter Chanel, a Frenchman who worked with sensitivity among the reformed cannibals of the Futuna Islands. He justified their welcome through ministration to the sick, but when his following increased and the chief's son sought to convert, Chief Niuliki ordered Chanel to be clubbed to death. This classic martyrdom is typical of the fate of many an idealistic missionary who, having disrupted the local balance of power by introducing a new belief was eventually murdered for his intrusive ideology. Chanel was the protomartyr of Oceania and is still especially honoured there and in Australasia.

89. *Above* **The Japanese Martyrs**

90. *Right* **St Jean de Breboeuf** (woodcut by Eric Gill)

In the two thousand years since St Paul's first journeys, evangelists have carried the Christian monastic tradition into every corner of the globe. History has been directly affected by their spreading of the Christian religious culture with more energy and conviction than that mustered by their competitors and predecessors. Their belief in the indispensably requisite nature of their faith and in universal salvation as the only alternative to damnation compelled them to travel huge distances to unknown places to preach their religious tenets to aliens. St Paul's example was followed by many dedicated missionaries who, despite dogmatism and fanaticism, may be regarded as the grand adventurers of Christianity, and whose daring has become a part of Christian folklore.

91. St Christopher (plastic statue) Recently demoted, he is the patron of travellers, as he was believed to have carried the Christ Child across a river.

Leaders and Heroes

In each period of Christian history popular cults emerged reflecting contemporary religious attitudes. Most of the early Christians were martyred, so their legends were full of bloodcurdling details. The medieval saints reflected the domination of the church in Europe. Sixteenth and seventeenth century saints spearheaded social and cultural changes while, in contrast, the eighteenth and nineteenth century saints were often pastel, pietistic figures who reaffirmed the church's resistance to the continuation of social changes which threatened its powers. Today Rome is trying to adapt the Church's image to suit a sceptical world which increasingly rejects traditional ideas of the miraculous but, paradoxically, remains hungry for signs of reassurance or an explanation of existence.

Every court has its jester and the saintly pantheon is no exception. The sixth century Syrian saint, Simon Salus, was called Simon the Crazy with good reason. He had spent some time as a hermit in Palestine before he returned to his birthplace, Homs, where by all accounts he behaved like Robin Hood as performed by the Marx Brothers. He tried to help the poor, especially harlots, by shoplifting provisions on their behalf. When not actively breaking the law he behaved publicly like a lunatic. Perhaps this was to prevent arrest, for some thought he was a charlatan or mad, while others accepted his conduct as appropriate in the ascetic tradition of being a fool for Christ's sake, and considered him a particularly convinced follower. The tradition of eccentric mendicants playing the part of roving village idiots started by Simon became prevalent among Orthodox Christians especially in Russia.

There, the sixteenth century saint Basil the Blessed performed as a traditional holy idiot and depleted the shops of Moscow in order to help those in need. He was either sufficiently devious or sufficiently mad to rebuke his Tsar, Ivan the Terrible, and escape punishment. He is commemorated by the extraordinary cathedral of St Basil which stands in Red Square in ironic juxtaposition to Gum, the biggest department store in Russia.

At the opposite end of the social and behavioural scale were the royal saints of Europe, in whom were joined political and religious power which deeply affected the development of their countries. English history is replete with saintly kings and queens. Amongst them St Edward the Confessor has been especially admired as an unassuming and Christian monarch. His marriage was reputedly unconsummated because of his chaste ideals. Edward was probably tricked by Duke William of Normandy into offering him hopes of the English succession, and the Norman Conquest was achieved within a year of his death. Edward was believed to have performed miraculous cures and was the first king to cure scrofula, 'the King's evil', by touch.

The Hungarian princess St Elizabeth was one of the rare female saints to be defined outside

92. St Elizabeth of Hungary distributing largesse to a beggar.

who beat her regularly about the face and body on his instructions, and was canonised in 1235, four years after her death.

In the sixteenth century the Jesuits were ruled by the great-grandson of Pope Alexander VI, St Francis Borgia – sometime Duke of Gandia – as Vicar-General. A generation later another princeling, St Aloysius Gonzaga, heir to the ruling house of Castiglione, became a model novice. An undoubted prig, Aloysius vowed chastity at the age of nine. Moved to extreme embarrassment by the revealing clothes worn by women at his father's court, he walked around with his eyes fixed firmly on the ground. Ever preoccupied with combatting his own sinfulness, he adopted an attitude of superior disdain for the frailties of others.

Perhaps the most famous victim of the medieval conflict between church and state was St Thomas à Becket, Archbishop of Canterbury, formerly Lord Chancellor of England and long-time intimate of Henry II. His lasting importance began with his death, the result of the deterioration of his friendship with the King. On his appointment as Primate, Thomas changed dramatically from having been Henry's rumbustious playmate to becoming his most severe critic. Confrontations over the areas of jurisdiction of the church and state were intensified by Henry's personal anger and confusion. Four of Henry's men overheard the famous royal rhetorical question and rushed to Canterbury to find the 'turbulent priest' who had so infuriated their king that he now demanded his death. The dreadful murder in the cathedral shocked Europe; Henry did public penance, and Pope Alexander III canonised Thomas three years after his death. His body was enshrined at Canterbury, which became one of the most important centres of pilgrimage in Europe. His tomb was the site of innumerable reported miracles; more than seven hundred were recorded within the first ten years of his death.

her sexual role. When she was twenty, her husband the Landgrave of Thuringia was killed during a crusade. Her brother-in-law succeeded him and it is said that he threw Elizabeth out into the snow with her child in her arms. She became a Franciscan tertiary under the guidance of her chosen mentor, the inquisitor Conrad of Marburg. She suffered his appalling regime, surrounded by companions

Another churchman who had to contend with Henry II's temper was St Hugh of Lincoln. An eminent Carthusian, Hugh joined the English Church from Grand Chartreuse at Henry's own request. After a time as prior of the charterhouse at Witham, which Henry had founded in reparation for Becket's murder, Hugh was instated as Bishop of Lincoln. His career was spent negotiating the usual problems of the parameters of church and state power with three consecutive kings. Hugh's ability to survive the royal fits of temper was impressive. In the face of Henry's notorious fury, he simply laughed; he deflated Richard the Lionheart by shaking him by the shoulders when he sulked; he persevered in advising and criticising John Lackland who, despite a marked indifference to Hugh's admonitions, volunteered to be a pallbearer at his funeral. Hugh's unusual concern for the rights of his parishioners and the lower orders of the clergy made him a much loved bishop, for most prelates lived like princes, isolating themselves as much as possible from the problems of their flock.

A later victim of the continuing struggle between great statesmen and whimsical kings was Sir Thomas More, who was honoured by both Protestants and Catholics as a political and religious martyr after his execution during the Reformation. Thomas was a humanist and a statesman of international repute and his life was the epitome of religious, cultural, political and personal success. A close friend of Henry VIII, a most enlightened monarch in his youth, he was created Lord Chancellor. Then, in 1534, the Act of Succession landed Thomas in a quandary. Henry remarried without the requisite papal annulment and then required his subjects to repudiate any foreign authority and swear allegiance to their king. Thomas flatly refused to deny the spiritual authority of the papacy and was imprisoned, tried and beheaded. Thomas More has been revered for his convictions for, fully

93. The statue of **St Dominic of Abruzzi,** who rid this Italian region of snakes, being processed in an annual ceremony, entwined with live snakes which are kept as pets for this occasion.

realising the disastrous implications of his stated beliefs, he defended himself ably and courageously at his trial and faced death calmly. He was sanctified for his martyrdom and his uncompromising devotion to his view of the essence of the spiritual role of the church.

A political victim of a different order was the French heroine Joan of Arc – a perennially

BIENHEUREUSE JEANNE d'ARC
PRIEZ POUR NOUS
1412   1431

fascinating and legendary figure, whose story is as familiar as it is incredible. A simple peasant girl persuaded the Dauphin of France that she was the very person to lead the French armies in the relief of Orleans from the English. She succeeded and commanded the French army in a series of victories until she saw the Dauphin crowned King at Rheims. Her spiritual 'voices' warned her that her death was near, but she battled on until captured by the Burgundians who sold her to the English. She was tried as a witch, condemned and burned at the stake in the market place in Rouen. Joan was only nineteen when she died and became her country's national heroine – a symbol of God's might and his protection of the nation. She was the best-known victim in French history and the mighty virgin warrior – an awesome combination.

Since time began people have followed leaders. To follow a leader is, at best, to follow an inspired example and the Christian saints were upheld as such examples. Their cults met basic and homely needs as well as more lofty aspirations. They provided reassurance in daily matters. The company of saints was, and remains for many, an institution which guarantees a safety-net to the sinner or perhaps an extra clause in the great insurance policy for life after death.

94. St Joan of Arc as the standard bearer at the coronation of Charles VII at Rheims Cathedral.

The publishers would like to thank the following people for their help and permission to reproduce illustrations numbered below:

Joanna Booth: 26
Bowes Museum, Barnard Castle, Co Durham: 15
Cooper-Bridgeman Library: 7, 12, 23, 27, 42, 44, 51, 64
Andrew Edmunds: 82
Fabbri: 6, 24, 28, 32, 34, 38, 39, 40, 45, 54, 65, 75
Giraudon: 2, 3, 13, 30, 33, 72, 78
Michael Fathers: 20
Keystone Press Agency: 36, 88, 93
Mansell Collection: 55
Christopher Mendez: 14
National Gallery, London: 11, 15, 18, 21, 22, 29, 41, 43, 53, 63, 70, 86
Private Collection, Paris: 52
Punch: 4
Scala: 8, 25, 37, 56, 73
Geoffrey Van: 9, 10, 80
Victoria and Albert Museum: 31, 90

Index

Figures in italics refer to illustration numbers

Agatha *34*, 39, 40
Agnes *32*, 38
Aloysius Gonzaga 108
Ambrose *40*, 47
Andrew *11*, *82*, 11, 14
Angela Merici 77, 89
Anthony the Anchorite *63*, *64*, 73, 75, 80
Audrey 53, 55
Augustine of Canterbury 7, *84*, 98, 99
Augustine of Hippo *41*, 48, 49, 50, 51, 66, 77

Barbara *26*, 34
Bartholomew *8*, 11, 14
Basil the Blessed 107
Basil of Caesarea *38*, 44, 49, 75
Bede 78
Benedict *66*, 75, 77, 78
Bernadette *62*, 70
Bernard of Clairvaux *68*, *70*, 49, 79, 80
Boniface 99
Brigid 39
Bruno *69*, 49, 80

Carlo Borromeo 75
Catherine of Alexandria *25*, 33, 34, 49
Catherine Laboure *61*, 69, 70
Catherine dei Ricci *57*, 66
Catherine of Siena *55*, 63
Cecilia *31*, 38
Christopher *91*
Claire *49*, 55, 85
Columba 96
Columban 96, 98
Cosmos *23*, 25
Cyril 99, 101

Damian *23*, 25
David *82*
Denis 25, 29
Dominic *71*, 80, 83, 85
Dominic of ??? *93*

Edward the Confessor 107
Elizabeth *92*, 107, 108
Eustace *24*, 30
Euctochium 77

Francis of Assisi *72*, 55, 80, 83, 85
Francis Borgia 108
Francis Xavier *87*, *88*, 101, 102

Genevieve *48*, 55
George *19*, *20*, *82*, 23
Gerard Majella *60*, 67, 69
Gregory the Great *44*, *83*, 50, 51, 98, 99
Gregory of Nazianzus 44, 49

Hugh of Lincoln 109

Ignatius of Antioch 30
Ignatius of Loyola *73*, 85, 87, 101

James the Greater *10*, 11, 13, 21
James of Jerusalem 11, 14
James the Lesser 11, 14
Jane de Chantal *78*
Januarius *4*
Japanese Martyrs 89
Jean de Breboeuf *90*, 102, 103
Jerome *42*, *43*, 33, 49, 50, 75, 77
Joan of Arc *94*, 110
John 11, 13, 15, 17, 21
John the Baptist 7, 8, 11, 14
John Bosco *79*, 92
John of the Cross 64, 66
John Chrysostom *39*, 44
John of God *74*, 87, 89
Joseph 14
Joseph of Arimathaea *3*
Judas Iscariot 11, 15
Jude 11, 14, 15
Julitta *30*

Lawrence *22*, 25
Lucy *29*
Luke *14*, *15*, 15 – 17

Margaret 34
Margaret Mary Alacoque *58*, 66, 67
Maria Goretti *35*, 40, 41
Marina de Jesus Paredes y Flores 58, 59
Mark *13*, 15, 16
Mary of Egypt 61
Martin of Tours *80*, 93, 95

Mary Magdalene *52*, *53*, 59, 61, 66
Matthew *12*, 11, 15
Matthias 11, 15
Methodius 99, 101

Pachomius 75
Paphnutius 61
Paul *14*, *15*, *37*, *65*, 11, 17, 21, 23, 43, 47, 49, 51, 93, 105
Paul of Thebes *65*
Paula 77
Patrick *81*, *82*, 95, 96
Pelagia 61
Peter Chanel 104
Bl Peter Sanz *85*
Peter (Simon the Fisherman) *21*, 11, 13, 14, 16, 21, 39, 59
Philip 11, 14
Philip Neri *54*, 63
Pius X *6*, 8

Romuald *67*
Rose of Lima *50*, 55 – 58

Sebastian *17*, *18*, 23
Simeon Stylites 77
Simon Salus 107
Simon the Zealot 11, 15
Stephen 23

Teresa of Avila *56*, 64, 66, 70
Thais **61**
Thomas 11, 14
Thomas Aquinas *45*, 51, 52, 70
Thomas à Becket 108
Thomas More 109

Uncumber 39
Ursula *27*, *28*, 34

Veronica *51*
Vincent Ferrar *86*
Vincent de Paul *76*, 69, 70, 89
Virgin Mary *46*, *47*, 11, 14, 34, 53, 59, 66, 69, 70, 77

Wilgefortis *33*, 39